MAKING SPACES
FOR COMMUNITY
DEVELOPMENT

Michael Pitchford

with Paul Henderson

This edition published in Great Britain in 2008 by

The Policy Press in association with the Community Development Foundation
University of Bristol
Fourth Floor
Beacon House
Queen's Road
Bristol BS8 1QU
UK

Tel +44 (0)117 331 4054
Fax +44 (0)117 331 4093
e-mail tpp-info@bristol.ac.uk
www.policypress.org.uk

British Library Cataloguing in Publication Data
A catalogue record for this book is available from the British Library.

Library of Congress Cataloging-in-Publication Data
A catalog record for this book has been requested.

ISBN 978 1 84742 259 0 paperback

Cover design by Qube Design Associates, Bristol
Front cover: image kindly supplied by www.alamy.com
Printed and bound in Great Britain by Hobbs the Printers, Southampton

Contents

Foreword

Community development has a long and rich history and this publication brings forth the experiences and insights of a group of experienced practitioners with a wealth of knowledge and insights that will help those of you who are practising community development today. The book provides a useful historical context for community development, the changing sponsors and focus for community development practice, from the late 1960s until the present day. I was particularly interested to read about the different approaches and tactics used by practitioners to effect change and in part how these have evolved over the years.

At the heart of community development is the principle of learning from practice and what better way to start than to reflect on the experiences of those who have been there and done it over many years. While the context for community development today is radically different to that of the late 1970s, I can see within these descriptions how many practice challenges are still topical: for example, the challenge to ensure that the community development approach is given space and time to realise the benefits for both communities and government.

The purpose of the publication is both to provide valuable insights, as well as kick-start a debate within the community development field, which we would like to work with our national partners to lead. In terms of profile, community development has received greater attention and focus in recent years. Nothing can be taken for granted, though, as increasingly our communities experience rapid and often unexpected change and community development practice has to be prepared and equipped to continuously respond to this. What is most important is that together with government and public sector agencies, community development is able to empower communities to achieve the positive changes they perceive as necessary. This book is a valuable contribution and catalyst to what I hope will be both a national discussion combined with local actions.

Alison Seabrooke
Chief Executive
Community Development Foundation

Community Development Foundation (CDF)

CDF is the leading source of intelligence, guidance and delivery on community development in England and across the UK. Our mission is to lead community development analysis and strategy to empower people to influence decisions that affect their lives.

CDF's key aim is to spread ways of building engaged, cohesive and stronger communities and a more effective community sector:

- by advising government and other bodies on community development
- by analysing policy to identify good community development practices
- by conducting research and evaluation
- by supporting community development work through networks, links with practitioners and work with partner organisations
- by managing funding schemes for local projects
- through training, events publications and consultancy.

We work with government departments, regional and local public agencies and community and voluntary sectors. We also operate at a European and international level. We are a non-departmental public body sponsored by Communities and Local Government (CLG) and a charity registered in England and Wales and recognised in Scotland.

Community Development Foundation
Unit 5, Angel Gate
320–326 City Road
London EC1V 2PT
Registered Charity Number 306130

Tel: 020 7833 1772
Fax: 020 7837 6584

Email: admin@cdf.org.uk
Website: www.cdf.org.uk/

Acknowledgements

I am indebted to many people who helped me from start to finish with the publication, in particular, Mick Hamilton at Laings who was willing to fund the initial idea. I want to thank all those individuals I interviewed to whom I'm so grateful for their generosity of time and patience with my questions. I learnt so much from listening to them and I hope they recognise their insights and reflections in what follows. Paul Henderson and Catriona May have been a continual support throughout; the publication would not have happened in the form it has without them. Alison Gilchrist, Marj Mayo, Beth Longstaff, Sal Hampson and Jill Bedford were kind enough to act as readers providing valuable and considerate feedback. Other friends and colleagues who have guided me to a clearer understanding include Melanie Bowles, Cara Macdowall, Jayne Humm, Jenny Fisher, Lesley Graham and Mae Shaw.

Last but far from least a huge gratitude to Sacramenta Rodrigues and John Stone for the endless administrative support they provide me with which allows me the luxury to wander off and interview practitioners from the past. To all those who've helped, challenged and argued – thank you.

ONE

Introduction

When I started in my first job as a community development practitioner, I assumed that community development was in its infancy, a completely new way of working. I was consumed by what was happening at the time, primarily what funding was available for the next project we had up our sleeve. Theory did not really figure in my work and in many ways we discovered for ourselves through trial and many errors, what others had already learnt a long time ago. We rolled up our sleeves, got stuck in and placed an emphasis on learning from those we worked with.

It was not until the project I worked within recruited an older worker with a community development background that it began to dawn on me that while our work was proving successful, it was not necessarily ground-breaking and perhaps we could be achieving much more. In her gentle and understated way, not to offend my sense of self-importance, this worker showed me how much of what we were doing had been done by her and many others back in the 1960s and 1970s. What obstacles had they faced? What paths did they take and what did they learn? Slowly a light turned on and I became intrigued at the thought of learning from those who had been working within communities for many years and relating this to my current practice.

There is no learning like learning from your own mistakes but what a wonderful resource there is in those who have been practising for many years.

Thus began the idea of interviewing experienced community development practitioners to extract their learning, experiences and insights and to relate these to present-day practice and contexts. What light, if any, could these reflections shed on current opportunities, dilemmas and tensions within community development?

What follows is an account of the key changes to the context and practice of community development since the 1970s, told through the experiences and insights of a group of highly experienced practitioners. The book is intended for those practising and interested in practising community development today, and is aimed at encouraging practitioners to think and reflect on their work. Ideally, it will contribute and in some cases kick-start debate within the field of community development. The book is not a history of community development, nor is it an attempt to analyse community development theory. It asks questions rather than gives answers and provides an opportunity to listen to the insights from previous practice and judge for ourselves if these contributions have something to tell us today.

First, a few words about how interviewees were identified. As with community development, it was largely common sense: advertisements in community development magazines, use of networks and key contacts and direct approaches to individuals whose names were recommended. The emphasis within our search was to focus on those with approximately 20-25 years of experience or more, and to ensure that each interviewee would be able to reflect back critically on their experiences. Thirty-three community development practitioners were identified with great depth and variety of experiences, and many had over 25 years of experience.

Those interviewed do not equally represent gender and ethnicity – 36% female interviewees and 18% black practitioners. We made use of black networks and tried to identify practitioners through black professionals in other fields, but were unable to identify any more practitioners from this earlier period. It was suggested that in the 1970s there were few black practitioners and most were involved as activists. What follows needs to be read in the light of this imbalance.

The combined experience of those practitioners interviewed totals over 800 years of practice from the late 1960s through to the present day. Experiences range across areas of play-work and youth through to the environment, community enterprise, 'race' equality, immigration and housing. Interviewees were evenly balanced between statutory and voluntary sector experiences and were spread around the country with two interviewees describing their work in Wales and three interviewees talking in the context of Scotland; we were unable to identify practitioners from Northern Ireland. The bulk of the experiences drawn on are from the perspective of neighbourhood-based community development, in which the worker had a generic role across a range of issues that today would be themed into the likes of housing, equalities, capacity building, training and so on.

While experiences and insights differed widely, each interviewee was keen not to appear nostalgic. If what follows reads as rose-tinted then that is my responsibility, as interviewees were trying to draw out their learning rather than harking back to what it used to be like. I was struck by the interest shown by interviewees and their generosity of time in being interviewed, for which I am extremely grateful. Each interview was packed with learning as I listened to different experiences and was left feeling both privileged yet panicked at the thought of having to recount these insights. The interviews gave voice to a diverse range of views from community organising and grass-roots action through to community development in the context of partnerships and service delivery. While I have not quoted from every interview, each one has influenced both myself and the points made in the book. I have not tried to take sides where views have differed, but simply tried to look at what is being said and its relevance in the light of practice today.

The book has six chapters. In Chapter Two, Paul Henderson provides a brief historical overview of community development over the past 40 years to act as a 'backcloth' for the experiences of the practitioners interviewed. Beginning in the 1960s with the dominance of social work and the appointment for the first time of community development officers within local authority social work departments, the chapter moves through the radical campaigns of the 1970s and the challenging reports from the community development projects (CDPs). Community development in the 1980s suffered significant cutbacks and there was a move away from social services departments as the 'sponsor' of community development towards that of economic development. This was developed further in the 1990s with the urban regeneration programmes in which community development became intertwined with the community involvement aspects of regeneration programmes. Community development in the 21st century has gained a higher prominence with a New Labour government that emphasised the role of the 'community' in improving public services and promoting local democracy, but has brought with it tensions around the lack of a community voice, which is vital for community development work to take place.

In Chapter Three, some of the key shifts in terms of the landscape of community development are highlighted, in particular the change from a confrontational approach to the model of partnership working which predominates in all areas of regeneration and urban renewal. Today, participation in the partnership model has brought with it a greater recognition of the potential role of community development in achieving policy objectives and thus the community development workforce has grown substantially. Practitioners are now required to be far more accountable for how they carry out their roles, although this accountability is upwards to the funder or authority rather than to the communities in question. The professionalisation of community development poses challenges for today's practitioners trying to combine a passion for social change and justice with their day-to-day practice.

In Chapter Four we begin to look at the fundamental questions of what community development is and why we are doing it. The chapter

—
3

describes the differing aims of 'well-being' and relationships, and social justice and equality, and discusses the tensions that have always existed within community development between differing interests and priorities. Community development today is focused very much on the well-being agenda and in the context of persistent poverty and rising inequalities we ask if community development can do more to connect with anti-poverty initiatives and social justice, or would that simply result in unfulfilled aspirations?

Chapter Five looks at the earlier confrontational approaches used by practitioners and contrasts this with the shift towards practice within a community planning framework. Within campaigning community work during the 1970s, the purpose of the community development role was to support local communities to challenge and make demands on the local state. Pressure was viewed as the way to achieving change. How do practitioners today go about achieving change and to what extent are conflicts between the interests of communities and the state avoided through a focus on 'engagement'?

In Chapter Six we look at the fundamental issue of accountability and its impact on community development practice and relationships between practitioners and communities. Upward accountability has increased considerably as part of the government's overall approach to driving up standards in public services. The resulting focus on programme outputs and targets is skewing practice away from empowerment and social change activity towards a greater emphasis on service delivery. The process of community development has also come under increasing pressure as the emphasis on short-term outputs does not fit easily with the sustained, long-term nature of community development. How have these changes impacted on the ability of practitioners to develop trusting relationships within the communities they work? Within the new policy context of neighbourhood decision making what opportunities exist for practitioners and communities to work together to exert greater influence and control within the setting of local priorities?

In the final chapter, Chapter Seven, we assess where community development is at today, try to identify the direction in which it is travelling and extract the key points of learning from the practitioner interviews as a way of guiding future discussions and decisions about community development. Community development is increasingly synonymous with engagement and involvement in order to meet the government priorities of public service reform and increased democratic participation. Sustained community development results in increased community involvement but this should neither be its starting point nor its end. To what extent is community development in the UK losing a sense of purpose and direction and becoming increasingly disconnected from its origins in social change?

Opportunities do exist in the current environment for community development to get back to what it does well, ensuring that communities have real voice and influence in the issues affecting their lives. In order to take advantage of these opportunities it requires that the community development field clarifies its vision and purpose. Community development must surely set goals for itself beyond the policies and programmes of the current government and begin to plan and organise itself in order to achieve these goals. The key message of this publication is that a debate needs to start within the community development field to review the current position and future directions for community development, to ensure that communities receive the support they need to achieve the changes they themselves identify.

TWO

Community development: historical overview

Paul Henderson

A number of commentators have pointed to the mistake of assuming that community development is a recent arrival on the professional, social movement and social policy scenes, whether this was following the election in 1997 of the first Blair government or the new horizons that opened up for community development at the end of the 1960s.

The starting point of the history of community development is a matter of debate; it certainly goes back more than 100 years. In the following overview we have chosen to go back as far as 1968. This is because our purpose is simply to provide a backcloth or 'map' for the changing practice of community development, which is the focus of the publication. The intention is to refer to the main signposts in community development, not to weigh up or discuss all the twists and turns that have been experienced. This overview is not designed to be comprehensive. Nor does it expand on the different social policy and political contexts. By keeping a focus on community development we hope to give the reader the essential background required for the book as a whole.

The danger of providing a narrative account is that the significance of underlying themes and developments will be missed. The interviewees referred to many of these. Three themes that have been particularly important are as follows.

Auspices: throughout most of its history, community development has turned to more powerful professions for support. It has needed a 'backer' or sponsor that could organise funding, employment and training. Community development has shifted from one sponsoring profession to another. Being aware of this process is important because it helps to explain why, at different points in time, community development took a particular direction. We refer to the different periods, which inevitably overlap with each other, in the course of the narrative.

Changing policy contexts: intertwined with the political imperatives, all of which had major implications for community development throughout the period, have been significant policy changes. A clear example was the decision of the Callaghan government in 1976 to comply with the economic requirements set out by the International Monetary Fund, followed by stringent public expenditure cuts. We shall see that, on a number of occasions, community development was forced to respond to major policy changes. The booklet by Taylor and West (2001) and the chapter by Marilyn Taylor on the changing context of UK practice (in Craig and Mayo, 1995) give a more expansive summary of this dimension of community development.

Responding to new ideas: the theory and practice of community development has been informed and influenced by new or re-fashioned ideas during the period. It is, of course, very difficult to gauge the extent of such processes. Community development, however, has always been interested in debating ideas and it is reasonable to assume that, in their different ways, they have been of critical importance. This is certainly true of black and feminist thinking during the 1970s and 1980s. Current ideas about civil society (Mayo, 2005) and social capital (Putnam, 2000) are undoubtedly impacting on community development.

The 1960s

The hold that the social work profession obtained over community development from the late 1960s stemmed from the thinking and writing of people such as Murray Ross and Eileen Younghusband. A working group chaired by Younghusband conceptualised community work as part of social work (Younghusband, 1959). Prior to this, it had been the education profession that had helped to support community development, particularly through the development of community associations and community centres (see Thomas, 1983).

The Seebohm Report (1968) set an operational framework for community work to be located in a social work context and this led, a year or two later, to community development officers being appointed by the new social services departments (social work departments in Scotland). 1968 was the key year for community development: 'If there was a "golden age" of community work it was the period from 1968 until the mid-to-late 1970s' (Popple, 1995, p 15). 1968 saw both the publication of influential reports and the emergence of government funding for community development. Previously, projects such as the North Kensington Family Study project in London had been predominantly in the voluntary sector. The Gulbenkian Report (see below) and the launch of the Urban Programme, the community development projects (CDPs) – planned in 1968 but announced in 1969 – and the Young Volunteer Force Foundation (YVFF) were the main new drivers of community development. The Calouste Gulbenkian Foundation played a significant encouraging role. The study group that produced the 1968 report (Calouste Gulbenkian Foundation, 1968), and a larger group that published a further report a few years later (Calouste Gulbenkian Foundation, 1973), brought together key individuals from the education and social work professions.

The Urban Programme proved to be a lifeline for many community groups for over 20 years. It was launched by the government in response to mounting anxieties about urban deprivation and the rediscovery of poverty, coupled with concerns about immigration and 'race'. The CDPs, which ran in 12 localities until 1977, exerted a strong influence on the community development profession at the time and later, because of their success in disseminating strong messages, based on evidence from most of the projects, about the causes of deprivation. YVFF was set up with the support of the three main political parties as part of the government's response to civil unrest.

The setting up of the Association of Community Workers (ACW) in 1968, preceded only two years earlier by the establishment of the *Community Development Journal*, was further evidence of community development having taken a quantum leap forward at this time. Two other reports gave an indication of the potential breadth of the profession: the Skeffington Report (1969) was aimed at planners and argued for the importance of public participation; and the Fairbairn-Milson Report (1969), reflecting the youth service's increased commitment to outreach and detached work, set youth work within the context of community development.

The 1970s

From the early 1970s, community development entered a phase of increased militancy. At a professional level this was reflected in the hard-hitting CDP reports giving a structural analysis of deprivation. At the grass-roots level, however, much of the action revolved around welfare rights campaigns and the organisations of tenants and residents on housing issues, particularly rent increases and anger at empty properties – action on the latter issue was led by the squatting movement.

At the same time community development expanded within the social work context, not only through the appointment of community development workers but also through the development of community social work: patch-based social work teams that set out to respond to community issues as well as individuals' problems. This development was discussed positively in the Barclay Report (1982). It was also at this time that the large childcare voluntary organisations such as The Children's Society and Barnardo's strengthened their use of community development principles and methods, especially when linked with family centres.

The foundations for the building of a strong basis for community development in Scotland were laid during the 1970s. One of the recommendations of the Alexander Report (1975) was that adult educators should adopt a community development approach and local authority education departments became the major employer of community development/community education workers. In addition, Strathclyde Regional Council, at the time the largest authority in the UK, placed community development at the centre of its anti-deprivation strategy.

As the decade advanced, feminist and black perspectives became increasingly significant influences on community development. On the one hand, they provided a new perspective on CDP's radical analysis of community development; on the other, they stimulated the growth of local action groups as well as groups and networks which shared a common interest or identity. The development of community health projects owed much to the influence of feminist thinking.

Unemployment became a dominant issue at the end of the 1970s and programmes launched by the government's Manpower Services Commission offered new, albeit controversial, opportunities for employing community development workers. There were wide-ranging debates within the community development profession on future scenarios for funding, training and employing community development workers, captured at a national conference organised by the ACW and the National Institute for Social Work in 1979, the same year that saw the election of the Thatcher government.

The 1980s

This decade is usually characterised as when community development, because of wide-ranging public expenditure cuts, was forced to defend itself. It was also the period when community development began to move towards economic development as its source of support. By the end of the decade the toehold that community development had secured in the social work sector was slipping away.

The radical, market-oriented changes introduced by the Conservative government threatened to leave community development in a state of confusion. This was compounded by the effects of economic recession towards the end of the decade. Yet government initiatives such as the Community Programme created community work posts and in both the statutory and voluntary sectors community work jobs were still being advertised. The Church Urban Fund, for example, set up following the *Faith in the city* report (Archbishop's Commission on Urban Priority Areas, 1985), provided job opportunities for church-based workers.

In 1983 the first national survey of community workers had shown there to be a total of 5,365 employed workers (Francis et al, 1984), and there is no evidence that this figure dropped significantly by the end of the decade. There was, undoubtedly, a sense of unease as well as an awareness of the difficulty of responding effectively to challenges such as those posed by riots in inner cities and by the future of coalfield communities following the miners' strike of 1984-85.

It was perhaps significant, therefore, that steps were taken towards the end of the 1980s to set up an umbrella organisation for community development, leading to the establishment of the Standing Conference for Community Development (later the Community Development Exchange or CDX) in 1991. The Federation of Community Work Training Groups (later the Federation for Community Development Learning or FCDL) was set up in 1982. A few years later the remit of the Community Projects Foundation (later the Community Development Foundation or CDF) was changed from that of being a fieldwork management organisation (the role it had played since it was launched as the YVFF) to being a support and dissemination organisation for community development. Thus the community development profession was getting itself better prepared both to see itself through difficult times and to respond effectively in expansionary periods.

The 1990s

The introduction of the government's City Challenge programme in the early 1990s began the process of drawing community development into the sphere of urban regeneration. This was partly because City Challenge, and subsequent programmes, required that there be community involvement and partly because regeneration was where the key policy making was taking place. There was a commitment to area-based approaches and capacity building. The various 'rounds' of the Single Regeneration Budget in England put increasing emphasis on community involvement, as did similar programmes in Scotland, Wales and Northern Ireland. These were the precursors of the New Deal for Communities and social inclusion programmes that were launched later.

The window of opportunity for community development became much more substantial following the election of the first Blair government in 1997. It should be noted, however, that important building blocks for community development were put in place earlier in the decade:

- CDF's new remit resulted in it developing policy-related research. A particularly important outcome of this was documentation of the community sector as a major component of the voluntary sector rather than as a small appendage to it (Chanan, 1992).
- In Northern Ireland, a major review of community development undertaken at the beginning of the decade led to a significant growth in the recognition of community development.
- In Scotland, the setting up of the Scottish Community Development Centre (a partnership between CDF and the University of Glasgow) in 1994 was of equal significance.
- In England, community development in local authorities was given a fillip by the publication of reports by the Association of Metropolitan Authorities (1989, 1993).
- Even community development in rural areas, for so long only a blip on the community development screen, began to expand.
- Europe had also started to figure in community development. It had been a source of funding for projects for a number of years, and the various Poverty Programmes had helped give community development a higher profile. In 1991 community development organisations from 11 countries formed the Combined European Bureau for Social Development, a support and dissemination network that continues today.

2000-08

Positive responses to CDX's *Strategic framework for community development* (2001) and the trends identified by the second UK-wide survey of community development workers undertaken in 2002-03 suggest that by the beginning of the new millennium community development was in an expansionary phase. CDX's strategic framework was widely welcomed because it set out clear community development principles and values. The survey provided a much-needed insight into the nature of the profession, drawing attention in particular to the lack of training and job stability as well as to the increased requirement for community development workers to support partnership working (Glen et al, 2004).

While some would say that community development has achieved increased recognition by becoming too dependent on government policies and funding, others would argue that it reflects the maturing of community development and a preparedness to work for change strategically. Certainly professional community development has strengthened its position in relation to government. This reflects the latter's insistence that community involvement or community engagement must form a key part of all regeneration, social inclusion and health improvement programmes. There have, therefore, been many opportunities for community development organisations to contribute to and influence the themes of community involvement and community engagement within government policy making. Work undertaken in 2003-04 on a framework for community capacity building made strong links with community development (Home Office, 2004). So too did the government's response to the riots in three northern towns in 2001: increasingly, community development was seen to be of crucial importance for the effectiveness of community cohesion programmes.

In 2005 CDF was commissioned by the Department for Communities and Local Government (DCLG, which became CLG in 2006) to assess the strengths and weaknesses of the community development profession and put forward proposals for strengthening the role it could play. The report, *The community development challenge*, provides an important benchmark for community development because it signals the extent to which community development, working alongside government, is presented now with enormous potential as well as pitfalls (CDF et al, 2006). Follow-up reports being published by CDF in 2008 on the management, governance, strategic and evaluation implications of *The community development* challenge are evidence of the significance being attached to the latter's ideas (see Bowles, 2008; Miller, 2008; Longstaff, 2008a, 2008b).

Five other developments or themes that stand out during the 2000-08 period are:

- A continuing emphasis on partnership working, not only between statutory, voluntary and community organisations but also between agencies which are working for empowerment – the National Empowerment Partnership, for example, is a programme which is active both nationally and regionally. It is supported by the CLG and aims to improve the quality, coordination and evidence of community empowerment across England (see www.cdf.org. uk/). The establishment in the regions of specific community development networks in 2007–08 is recognition of the importance of the regional dimension of the partnership imperative, both for government policy and for practitioners and community groups.

- A growing research and practice literature that provides evidence that it is possible to evaluate community development rigorously. The impact of the evaluation models Achieving Better Community Development (Barr and Hashagen, 2000) and LEAP (Barr and Dailly, 2008) have been considerable.
- Sustained commitment to expanding community development training opportunities, especially for grass-roots practitioners and for experienced local people, through the National Occupational Standards (FCDL, 2002).
- Signs that the environmental agenda is impacting on the thinking and planning of community development organisations. For example, under Every Action Counts, which is a voluntary and community sector programme, the FCDL is being funded to insert sustainable development into community development training. It is also interesting to note that arguments over the government's plans to establish a number of eco-towns are as much about the social and community implications of the towns as about transport, housing and economic viability.
- An increased profile for rural community development. The decision of the Carnegie UK Trust in 2004 to set up its Commission for Rural Community Development was a reflection of this trend. The Commission reported in 2007 but the Trust has made a long-term commitment to supporting rural community development (see Carnegie UK Trust, 2007).
- The continuing impact, particularly in East London, of the Community Organising movement.
- Maintenance of a high standard of critical analysis of community development, notably in the publication by Margaret Ledwith (2005), and a willingness to explore theoretical issues (see, for example, the volume by Hugh Butcher et al, 2007).

The lifeblood for effective community development depends on the energy and commitment of local people. In a decade which is presenting new dilemmas as well as opportunities for community development, this key component remains demonstrable: putting in long hours on partnership boards, setting up community enterprises, responding to racism and the tactics of racist political parties. These have been some of the actions of local people that re-affirm the dynamism and relevance of community development.

Community development 1960s–2000s

	1960s	1970s	1980s	1990s	2000s
PROJECTS AND PROGRAMMES	North Kensington Family Study Project started (1964); Young Volunteer Force Foundation launched (1968); Launch of Urban Programme (1968); Community Development Project (Home Office) began (1969)	Manpower Services Commission; Influence of women's movement and race	Community Health Projects	Community Organising in the UK started; City Challenge; Urban programme ends; Single Regeneration Budget; New Deal for Communities	
REPORTS	Gulbenkian Report (1968); Seebohm Report (1968); Fairbairn – Milson Report (1969); Skeffington Report (1969)	Gulbenkian Report (1973); Alexander Report (1975)	Barclay Report on Community Social Work (1982); Faith in the city (1985); Community development: The local authority role (1989)	Community development in Northern Ireland? Perspectives for the future (1991); Local authorities and community development: A strategic opportunity for the 1990s (1993)	A new commitment to neighbourhood renewal (2001); The community development challenge (2006)
PROFESSION	Community Development Journal established (1966); Association of Community Workers founded (1968)		Federation of Community Work Training groups set up (1982); First UK-wide Survey of Community Workers (1983)	Standing Conference for Community Development established (1991); Scottish Community Development Centre set up (1994)	Strategic Framework for Community Development (2001); Second Survey of Community Workers (2003)
PERIODS	Education	Social work	Economic development	Regeneration/neighbourhood renewal	

THREE

A seat at the table? The changing context for community development

Community development can be heard echoing through much government rhetoric on communities. New Labour came to power in 1997 with a commitment to building strong communities and their third term manifesto talked of putting power and resources in the hands of the 'law-abiding majority'. There are more resources than ever for community-level activity and communities themselves are being positioned to have a central role in decision making within their neighbourhoods. David Miliband MP, for a short time the Secretary of State for Communities and Local Government, spoke of the double devolution of power from central government to local government, and from local government to citizens and communities in which he envisaged a vital role for small community groups (Miliband, 2006). The recent Local Government and Public Involvement in Health Act 2007 makes engagement with citizens a statutory duty and emphasises the need to involve the 'hard-to-reach'. I should be jumping for joy or clearing my desk, then, as surely our job is done. Communities should now be able to influence government policy and resourcing decisions directly, based on their own needs and experiences. Has it really ever been this good?

Relationships between community development workers and the state

The context for community development in the UK today is one in which communities are expected to participate within numerous 'partnerships' made up of statutory, voluntary and sometimes private sector 'stakeholders'. The theory behind such partnerships is that through working together we can achieve more for those communities that experience social exclusion and deprivation. It is felt that the partnership approach symbolises a more mature era in working relationships across sectors and it has come to define almost every recent government programme from education and health through to neighbourhood renewal and housing.

Looking back about 25 years ago to the late 1970s, partnerships and even joint working were scarce. Practitioners kept largely to themselves and there was little evidence of practitioners working in any formal manner with statutory departments or the private sector. Confrontation and conflict seemed to prevail rather than a more cooperative approach to the work. Dave Vanderhoven, a community and youth worker in Newham during the late 1970s, recalls his working relationships:

> 'I don't remember partnerships and multi-agency working. It was even rare for youth workers to work together.'

In the main, the relationship between community development workers and the state was not one of joint working and collaboration but more often one of conflict and antagonism. Practitioners felt it easier to distance themselves from a Conservative government that was seen as actively attacking deprived communities. Contrast this with the Labour government of today that has put communities high up on its agenda and has embraced the voluntary and community sectors as pivotal to revitalising public services and increasing democratic participation.

The environment in the late 1970s and early 1980s was politically tense, with many areas experiencing large-scale unemployment and the subsequent hardships that resulted from closures within major heavy industries such as coal, steel and the dockyards. Immigration and nationality were highly politicised issues, as they are today, and in the early 1980s a number of cities in England experienced widespread rioting linked to tensions around racism and immigration.

A strong feminist movement for gender rights was growing alongside the development of anti-racist theory and practice. At an Association of Community Workers (ACW) conference in the late 1970s, women began to critique how community development ignored women's community action. ACW subsequently established a women's caucus and organised four annual conferences on the issue of women and community work. At one of these conferences the women's caucus put up various resolutions about the involvement of women and Georgina Webster, a community worker in Lambeth at the time, recalls how this was received:

> 'This caused an incredible furore. Men in ACW, and even some women, were saying "this is not the way to do things".'

Georgina also recalls that at the same conference, Gus John, a guest speaker on 'race' and community work, drew interesting parallels between 'race' and the women's caucus, which posed serious challenges to the theory and practice of community development.

Within this environment there was also the emergence of new language and ideas, which for practitioners was both exciting and challenging. Practitioners used words such as 'needs', 'enabling' and 'organising', a more straightforward language than the language of corporate management that we adopt today.

> 'We certainly didn't talk about capacity building, networking
> and social enterprise.' (Charlie Jordan)

The language used related to a belief in a 'bottom–up' approach whereby needs, issues and opportunities were identified by practitioners and the communities in which they worked and then used to persuade funders, whether they be statutory or charitable trusts, to fund what it was the community wanted to do. Contrast this with today's language of 'capacity', 'engagement' and 'active citizens', which reflects the more centrally directed approach in which communities and community groups carry out activities and programmes in line with government priorities. Does the language we use today also affect the ways in which practitioners and communities think about community work, what is possible and how this can be achieved?

During the 1980s a number of changes occurred which began to impact significantly on community development and the way it was practised. On the one hand, the collective nature of society from which community development drew its strength began to be eroded under the Thatcher administration, the Prime Minister famously claiming there is "no such thing as society". Collective action, a cornerstone of community development during the 1970s, was distrusted by the government and came under attack as the 'personal choice' agenda came on stream. Individualised packages of care and the marketisation of increasing aspects of our lives made efforts at collective activities increasingly difficult.

Practitioners largely remembered the 1980s as a period of hostility for community development. Charlie Jordan, a community development practitioner in Brighton over many years, recalls there being just one community worker in Brighton, himself, and one community worker in Hove employed by the social services department. Social services was neighbourhood based and the commitment to community development that there was at the time was towards community social work:

> 'I would say that I and one or two others were only there because we believed that we were standard bearers for community development through the 1980s through a period of hostility to community development. We were holding the torch for something which would have perished in the South East had it not been for one or two people like us.' (Charlie Jordan)

Another influence on the practice of community development during the 1980s was an attack by the Thatcher administration on the role and functioning of local government. Local authorities were hit hard by a central government determined to curb expenditure and keep inflation low. Some local authorities began to see a potential power base within communities themselves and began to reach out to these communities. Local government thus became interested and receptive to a different way of working in which local voluntary and community organisations worked in partnership with the councils to achieve what they saw as common goals. This manifested itself in the establishment of community development departments within a number of local authorities. This was, in a sense, a forerunner of the current government drive for decentralisation, but ran aground as local authority powers and the scope for local innovation were increasingly undermined by regulations imposed from Whitehall.

A key element within this move towards a partnership approach and the subsequent inclusion of community development as a 'stakeholder' came from practitioners themselves. For some practitioners, the changes around this period resulted in significant shifts in their thinking and practice. Jerry Smith, working in Broxtowe as part of a large community development project in Nottingham, began to realise that there was mileage to be had in working with the local authority from the start rather than simply supporting the community to present their demands to the council or march on the town hall:

> 'The change for me was that I thought that there was a better chance of the community achieving what they wanted by engaging right at the beginning in the thought process with service providers, hearing what it was like to be a probation officer, a housing manager or a social worker and discussing that, understanding that perspective and equally, the professionals understanding more about what it was like from the residents' point of view and the

service users' point of view and getting a dialogue going.
It was like a win–win situation.' (Jerry Smith)

This new approach adopted by Jerry and others was significant in its emphasis on dialogue and mutuality in which authorities and communities would meet somewhere in the middle. This resulted in tensions and conflicts not just within the Nottingham project but also across the community development field as a whole, challenging the emphasis within community development on supporting bottom–up community campaigns. Many of these tensions still play themselves out today, although they are somewhat suppressed, as many workers feel that through partnerships they are being told to implement a national policy agenda on communities, rather than facilitating the experiences and views of communities into the planning of policy and design of funding programmes. Community development in this sense has diverted its focus from the politics of communities to the policies of government.

Within the partnerships of today, however, it is hoped there is space for communities to negotiate and influence where none has existed before. Practitioners may have more room for manoeuvre than initially appears to be the case. Communities have a place at the table to which they were not previously invited.

A common thread that runs from the mid-1970s to the mid-1990s is the peripheral role of community development other than perhaps in Scotland where, in authorities such as Strathclyde, community development was a significant component of the local authority infrastructure. In 1989, the social work department in Strathclyde Council employed 189 community workers (Barr, 1996). Community development has always tended to be somewhat invisible as communities rightly take the credit for any achievements. As a result, community development has had a low profile at a policy level in local and central government and is often misunderstood. During these years, community development tended not to be core to the work of a local authority and practitioners describe how community development was passed from department to department as part of continual local authority reorganisation:

'From the mid-1980s up till probably the middle of the 1990s it was a constant changing of departments and with that you get subtle changes in focus. We started in public relations, then community grants, equalities and then that was really the death-knell for community development from the council's point of view. When they were reorganising and deleting department by department, you sensed they didn't know what to do with you, so they would tag you on to the end of something.' (Christine Dixon)

Emerging policy today relating to local government, places local authorities centre stage in the push to improve and devolve services. A recognition that centralised policy making is not working has resulted in the boosting of the neighbourhood and devolution agendas. Local authorities will be the control mechanism for community development and its funding. At the same time, the role of local authorities is changing into one of commissioner, rather than providers, whereby they contract others to provide services. This is resulting in an ever-expanding role for consultants and the private sector that is likely to undermine the espoused aims of democratic control and public accountability. These may require community development to review once again its role and remit within the new context and to begin to forge new relationships and ways of working.

During the 1980s and into the 1990s community development continued to suffer cutbacks and a significant degree of isolation. Brian Astin, who worked as a community development practitioner for the Barton project in Oxford, reflects on what happened:

'I think probably two things happened in tandem; local authorities during the 1990s got cash-squeezed and community development was not seen necessarily as a core activity. It was seen as an activity that staff other than just purely community development staff could undertake. Alongside that, I think there was the trend in a lot of the other professions to focus in much more tightly on core activities.'

Professions such as social work and youth work focused on direct work, and Brian recalls how the preventative nature of community development was pulled back. Disturbances in the northern towns of Bradford, Oldham and Burnley in 2001 and more recently in Birmingham have resulted in a government quest for 'community cohesion', for which community development is seen by some practitioners as a vital ingredient to avoid future disturbances. However, as memories of these particular disturbances fade and slip off the political priority list, the harder it may become for community development in this context to rely on the funding needed to help rebuild divided and deprived communities.

Community development today is increasingly emphasising the methods of involvement and engagement and disseminating these techniques for use by other professionals such as the police, planners and architects. While interest, awareness and understanding of how to involve communities is clearly a good thing and will surely make for better public services, are there underlying assumptions that anyone can do community development or even that community involvement and community development are one and the same?

Impact of the partnership climate

The combination of a Labour government championing 'community', receptivity to partnership working on the part of local authorities and practitioners pursuing dialogue rather than confrontation has resulted in community development coming in from the cold in a way that it has not done since the Labour government sponsored the Community Development Project (CDP) in the late 1960s. Community development is on the brink of much wider recognition as a process for bringing about positive change within communities. But what has inclusion of community development within the partnership model meant for practice, practitioners and communities?

In terms of numbers of designated posts, the community development profession has expanded rapidly in recent years. Today it is estimated that there are 20,000 full-time community development workers (Glen et al, 2004) across England. Back in the mid-1970s, Jerry Smith remembers:

> 'There were probably not more than four hundred community workers nationally, and I knew about half of them personally.'

Alan Barr, an influential practitioner and academic in Scotland who at the time worked for Oldham CDP, recalls:

> 'We were all in touch with one another. Had we the kind of networking capacity we have got now, it would have been easier but there was always somebody who was working on something similar and so that capacity to network and to use other people's knowledge was there. People were

supplying stuff to each other and that was an important part
of the skills that were there.'

Practitioners were swapping information, resources, contacts and
experience and these became important elements within the mix of
skills and expertise that practitioners had at their disposal. While there
are many more workers today, paradoxically, a common complaint of
practitioners is that of isolation, both within their agency and from
other practitioners in the field. Surveying the current landscape, Jerry
Smith observes:

> 'The contact between community development workers on
> a regular basis across the country, or even across a town, a city
> or a county just doesn't seem to happen any more. People
> are off working their own little corner. They may, if they are
> lucky, have a colleague or two to work alongside. If they're
> unlucky they'll be working on their own. They're working
> within the context of an agency for whom community
> development is a small part of their business. It seems to be
> atomised and doesn't hang together as it once did.'

Practitioners struggle to justify the time and resources to meet with
other workers. Does this lack of time, resulting from an increased
emphasis on targets and delivery, prevent practitioners within such
networks establishing the connections and depth with one another
that was fostered in earlier years in order to challenge and support
each other's practice?

The mutual support and advice exchanged between practitioners in
earlier years contrasts sharply with descriptions of consistently poor or
non-existent management of community development practitioners.
Managers rarely had a background in community work or community
development and were far more likely to have been social work
managers or from a probation background:

> 'I would honestly say that none of the managers had any
> community development background so you would never
> have dreamed of going to them to talk about the work.'
> (Christine Dixon)

> 'I was managed by somebody with no experience of
> community work and that was absolutely typical at that
> time.' (Georgina Webster)

The importance of a manager who understands what you are doing as a practitioner or at least, if they do not understand, allows the practitioner to get on and do the work, is key. Practitioners are considerably more successful in their efforts where a manager takes the role of shielding the practitioner and allowing her or him to practise while political negotiations and fundraising happen behind the scenes:

> 'I made the mistakes for those community workers to survive in a climate in which they would have otherwise perished. I kept them there because I was a good negotiator and good fundraiser.' (Charlie Jordan)

Poor management continues to plague the practice of community development today (but see Miller, 2008); at the same time, the Survey of Community Development Workers in the UK highlighted that practitioners themselves spend considerably more hours each week engaged in fundraising and monitoring activity which takes them away from work with communities (Glen et al, 2004).

The considerable increase in the number of community development practitioners is part of a new context for community development in which much greater dependence on government funding and thus closer ties to policy also feature. This has impacted significantly on the accountability of community development workers. During the 1970s and 1980s, practitioners were offered little direction or guidance and were similarly not required to account for their work in any detailed or formal manner:

> 'Community workers to an extent did what they liked, which meant there could be very good practice. It was great for me as an individual community worker because I had a huge amount of freedom to work on whatever issues came up, but in terms of any quality checks on my work, there were very little.' (Ann Chapman)

There was little accountability but a tremendous amount of freedom and scope for individual and collective initiative. While there may have been less money available for projects and activities than there is today, the climate was one of creativity and a more carefree environment. David Robinson, founder of Community Links, an inspiring social action centre in Canning Town, East London, recalls the spirit of the time:

'Community Links began with activities on a double-decker bus that we ran when we were at school. We would sometimes get 120 to 140 kids on and around the bus and the bus was really a bus without any seats; it was a very crude conversion indeed. The idea that we could do that now as 16 to 17-year-olds with 140 kids on the street! I don't know who would close us down first, the police or the Charity Commission.'

Today practitioners are working within a more constrained environment. There is a sense that practice has become more 'professional' and safe. Play schemes, for example, are not run by local parent groups from their homes or borrowed premises in the way they were 20 years ago, due to all the rules and regulations that surround this type of activity. Now they have become increasingly professionalised and bureaucratic. Reflecting on these changes, David Robinson identifies a need for a greater level of trust and discretion:

'Trust that once you've spotted somebody as a funder you assess carefully who is capable of delivering a scheme. Your managers trust you to make that judgement. You trust that organisation to deliver it to a far greater degree than we see at the moment. I think the burden of proof these days is for the applicant group to prove that it's not a bunch of paedophiles that will run off with the money. The assumption is you're both those things and you've got to prove that you're not. It ought to be the other way round a bit more and we've lost the balance on a lot of that. I'd like to see much more trust and discretion, recognising that sometimes, as ever with risk, that will mean things go wrong but if you eliminate all risk you eliminate all progress as well.'

Changes have also occurred in settings for practitioners and their proximity to the communities in which they work. Not all but some practitioners actually lived on the estates in which they worked as part of the community:

'My wife and I lived on the estate in Wolverhampton where I had my first job. A council house in the middle of the estate and we were on duty 24/7.' (Jerry Smith)

Bob Holman, a neighbourhood community worker and academic, together with his family, made a similar choice to live on the Southdown Estate in Bath (and 10 years later in Easterhouse in Glasgow). Having been involved on the committee of the Handsworth Adventure Playground in Birmingham while working as a lecturer in social work, Bob recalls travelling in from a suburb at the weekend to the adventure playground:

> 'The local black people started to call me a white missionary because I was travelling in. It made me think about the essence of community work and that they [the community] had much more respect for people who lived there.'

For Bob the realisation was that:

> 'The most useful thing that new professionally trained people or anybody else could do was not to be a social worker that commuted in and out, as I'd done, but one that was actually on the spot.'

In both Southdown and Easterhouse, Bob played a professional role dealing with issues such as welfare rights, yet he was also a neighbour:

> 'It's very different. I think you've got to have almost a new concept. I call it "resourceful friend". You're both a person with certain skills and resources that most local people haven't got, but you're also a friend.'

Bob's approach was not the norm but is a challenging model of practice for us all. Living alongside those in need is most commonly practised by faith-based workers and has often been linked to funding from the Church Urban Fund for community projects. There are still faith-based community projects that pursue this approach such as the Eden project that works with young people in deprived communities in the North West of England, living alongside them and being there on a 24/7 basis. While for some practitioners there were undoubtedly pressures around boundaries and privacy, working in such a way gave practitioners first-hand experience and knowledge of the issues that needed to be addressed. Practitioners who lived and worked within communities often identified strongly with the community. This sometimes made it harder to adopt a more objective and once-removed role that is required within today's partnership structures.

So who were the practitioners of the 1970s and 1980s and how has this altered, if at all? Many of those practising community development in the 1970s and 1980s were politicised individuals who saw a close connection between their politics and their community work. They were driven by community development as a type of social movement, which was about achieving social change. Ros Abbott, a practitioner with experience both in England and Scotland over many years, describes her peers during the late 1970s and 1980s:

> 'Community development workers had very strong political views. That's why they were doing that work. They were in it because they wanted to see change, so the debates were about how you're practising community work and how you challenge power.'

However, these were not the only practitioners, as Alan Barr highlights:

> 'There were actually two strands. There was that group of people who were quite radicalised by their broader political experience at the time who saw community work as a means of expressing the values that they had established for themselves. But there was also, and always has been, a stream of community work that stretches right back to the community associations movement which was very much about providing leisure and educational opportunities in communities, which we had nothing to do with. I hardly knew it existed.'

These different strands in community development are evident in today's discussions and debates about community development and are reflected in the growing numbers of voluntary and community groups operating within the UK.

With the growth in the number and type of community development posts over the past few years have come new professionals who are not connected in the same way to the idea of community development as being part of a social movement for change and thus do not exhibit the same priorities and concerns:

'I look back at the people who I rate most highly. They weren't people who came into this as a kind of career. They were people who were driven by a set of values that they wanted to express in a way in which they work in communities. There are still a lot of those people around but as a proportion of the total number, as that number has grown, it is not necessarily that large. That's because what we've got now is an approach which sees community development much more as a profession.' (Alan Barr)

For those new practitioners who do enter the 'professional' community development field with a passion for social change, particularly those individuals who have worked as community activists within their area, they will soon face difficult choices and dilemmas as they come to realise that the focus to much of their work is around the implementation of national policy and targets within their locality, as described above. The question is whether they are able to achieve the changes with and for the communities they support that gives them a sense of purpose and worth.

Community development is certainly 'on the radar' in a way that it has not been before, and is referenced and recognised in a number of current policy initiatives and programmes of work from government. It is not under attack in the way it was in the 1980s and a burgeoning number of community development workers are active in all major policy themes, from citizenship and democratisation through to health and housing.

'There are the opportunities there. In the Safer and Stronger Communities Fund there is the capacity building dimension. There is the neighbourhoods element of it which talks about community work really. That is a fantastic opportunity and here is potentially more money around now than there ever was for community development work.' (Mandy Wilson)

The climate of partnership provides opportunities for communities and community development practitioners to work with service providers and influence policies and programmes, but these opportunities need to be taken, not declined for fear of disagreeing and thus being put back out in the cold. We need to ask ourselves whether there are costs to receiving such recognition and evaluate whether they are worth bearing. Is community development changing as a result and what might this mean for communities and those who practice community development?

FOUR

Can we do more? Assessing the purpose and role of community development

What is community development and why are we doing it? Fourteen years of practice and I am still having conversations about these very questions. I have not had a good enough understanding to clearly and convincingly explain the answer to someone in the street. Many other practitioners, past and present, have expressed similar confusions. This is not an accident. Community development is a practice which has been 'contested' for many years and there are strong claims from policy makers, practitioners and communities for what they understand and want it to be.

Having described the changing context for community development in the previous chapter, we focus in this chapter on the fundamentals of community development: what practitioners are trying to do, why and how. It is important to do this in order to assess the role that community development practitioners play today. We begin by discussing the differing aims of community development on which practice has focused. Tensions exist over the aims and we highlight how these tensions have been played out, exploring the role that values have had in assisting practitioners to manage contradictions and dilemmas. We then outline the key approaches to work with communities and look in particular at the period of the Home Office community development project (CDP), and how this affected subsequent practice. The chapter concludes with a discussion on the training that is provided for community development practitioners and how successful it has been in offering to practitioners what they need to deal with the contradictions inherent in their practice.

To locate the reader in the late 1960s, I have chosen to refer to a seminal report of that time, *Community work and social change* (Calouste Gulbenkian Foundation, 1968), usually referred to as the Gulbenkian Report. Funded by the Calouste Gulbenkian Foundation, the report was the product of a two-year study into the nature and extent of community work, carried out by a group of academics and administrators. While there were other reports to which we could contrast the role of community development, for example, the Seebohm

Report (1968), the Gulbenkian Report is widely regarded as a key driver for community development. It put community development on the policy and professional map, although the language and beliefs contained within the report were not wholly compatible with the thinking and views of many practitioners at the time.

Describing community development

Within the language and literature of community development today, the terms 'community work' and 'community development' are often used interchangeably. Community work is generally used to describe the 'work' done within communities focused around change and development. Community work suggests an occupation and links closely with the national occupational standards for community development work. Community development, on the other hand, is described by Henderson and Thomas as a distinct 'process of change and development that takes place in communities' (Henderson and Thomas, 2002, p 3), something that does not necessarily have to be done by workers.

To complicate matters, Community Development Exchange (CDX) defines community development as 'an occupation (both paid and unpaid) which aims to build active and influential communities based on justice, equality and mutual respect' (CDX, 2006). The Federation for Community Development Learning (FCDL) defines the purpose as 'to collectively bring about social change and justice, by working with communities…' (FCDL, A summary of good practice standards for community development work). More recently, *The community development challenge* (CDF et al, 2006) defines community development as:

> … a set of values embodied in an occupation using certain skills and techniques to achieve particular outcomes or provide an approach used in other services or occupations.

For me to get a handle on this and to be clearer and more succinct for my friend in the street, I can see that community development is:

- a process (not a one-off intervention);
- achieving change within and for communities to problems that they themselves identify (it is not about keeping things as they are and it is not top-down);

- focused on changes that will be about achieving greater equality, justice and respect;
- a collective process and done with (not for or to) communities;
- a process that can be done by volunteers and activists as well as paid professionals.

What is it all about?

So when I am asked why we do community development, presumably it is about achieving the type of social changes referred to above – equality, justice and respect? This is certainly the view of some of the practitioners interviewed during this work:

> 'It was about working with different people, deprived people to achieve change in their lives with that change coming from themselves.' (Georgina Webster)

> 'There were quite a lot of people who were driven by community development as something of a social movement. There was a sense that we were engaging with something that was fundamentally about social change.' (Alan Barr)

Although, looking back again to the Gulbenkian Report, it described the essence of community work somewhat differently, as:

> ... an effort to relate factors making for change in society to the inherent general needs of persons including their need for stable and congenial relationships with other persons. In pursuit of this general goal it may often be necessary to help people to press for such practical aids to well being as better housing, better working conditions, and higher standards of living. (Calouste Gulbenkian Foundation, 1968, p 80)

This use of the phrase 'well-being' relates to an emphasis within community work on promoting personal relationships within communities, what is often referred to within today's language as social capital and seen as key to community development practice. But why do relationships matter? It is believed that through developing contacts and relationships between community members, they will in turn work together to make their communities better places in which to live. The revival of the idea of 'neighbourliness' is part of this strand of thought, that good relations with those who live around you will improve the quality of life for people, lead to happier and healthier lives where we feel both safer and a greater sense of belonging. David Thomas has suggested that community work promotes 'communal coherence' through the development of relationships which enables communities to cope better with collective stress through recognising and talking about common problems and developing positive action to manage the stresses (Thomas, 1983, p 96). Relationships and social networks enable communities to share information, make sense of their experiences and articulate common needs and are seen as a prerequisite and are critical for community participation (Gilchrist, 2004).

However, the Gulbenkian Report suggested another intention behind the fostering of relationships within communities:

> It is as "felt" members of interdependent communities that persons experience social control with relatively little fuss, relatively little tension and maximum informality, gaining thereby within themselves knowledge of the measure of conformity expected of them and in what directions and how far they may exercise divergent initiative. (1968, p 80)

In this explanation, through focusing on relationships and relating to the changes taking place in society, community development ameliorates the more damaging and destructive effects of economic change, felt particularly by poor and disadvantaged communities, keeping the peace through relationships and self-help and avoiding the breakdown of community life in the context of high levels of unemployment and poverty. Community development in this scenario is about helping to integrate people into the norms expected by society and can be seen to be more about control and stability of deprived communities than change or development. In the words of Seymour Martin Lipsett, the role is to 'tidy up the ragged edges of the good society' (quoted in Shaw, 2004).

Today, government funding accounts for approximately 70% of all community development resources (Glen et al, 2004). *The community development challenge* (CDF et al, 2006) estimates there are currently 20,000 professional practitioners around the UK. While it is difficult to compare like with like, the Survey of Community Workers carried out in 1984 (Francis et al, 1984) identified a much smaller number of practitioners – 5,365 community workers in the UK with a further

291 community work managers. This same survey found that central government funded 30% of community work posts with a further 20% coming from the Urban Programme (joint local government/central government funding).

These figures represent a significant growth in government funding for community development and with such a level of dependency on statutory funding, government views on the role and purpose of community development carry considerable weight and influence. The Labour government sees community development as having a key role to play, in reviving low levels of democratic participation twinned with a vision to devolve local government services and functions down to the neighbourhood level. For example, community development underpins *Firm foundations* (Home Office, 2004), the government's plan to support community capacity building, in which community development is singled out as one of six core principles defining the plan.

Today's language of involving and empowering individuals and communities to influence services and become active in civil society has become the basis on which community development operates. Underpinning this language are the concepts of citizenship, facilitating service delivery by the voluntary and community sectors through capacity building these organisations and promoting self-help among deprived communities. Facilitating relationships within communities remains key to many of these tasks and is a core part of work to build 'cohesive' communities in the aftermath of the 2001 disturbances in the northern towns of Bradford, Oldham and Burnley.

Community development practice today is oriented towards the well-being agenda and much less is talked about its relevance to anti-poverty and social justice. According to the government's own statistics, 12.4 million people are still living in poverty, far higher than the figure of 15% of households in 1981 (DWP, 2004). According to the audit of social injustice (Paxton and Dixon, 2004), persistent poverty (defined as those living at least three years out of the last four years in poverty) remains 'stubbornly high' compared to the rest of Europe, with 11% of UK citizens living in persistent poverty compared to a European Union (EU) average of 9% and much lower figures of 5% in the Netherlands and 6% in Germany and Norway. The same report highlights widening income and wealth inequalities and declining social mobility. In this context, is the focus on well-being and relationships enough or do community development practitioners have more to offer?

The following two chapters outline the focus and activities of community development, past and present. While practice in the past appears to have had a greater focus on anti-poverty, equality and justice, it is questionable how appropriate and effective this was:

> 'There were so many problems and it was expected that community development work would solve a lot of these problems of poverty, etc. The whole thing was so vast. Community workers found it really hard to do that because they were overwhelmed with the problems locally.' (Ros Abbott)

While articulating aims of justice and equality, the community development field is wary about promising to make advances on poverty and inequality that it cannot deliver. Perhaps focusing on involvement and well-being, which has made significant gains in terms of improving local services for communities, offers a more realistic measure of change or perhaps we are selling ourselves short? Let us leave the final word on this to Charlie Garratt:

> 'I suppose it's whether it's about change. Workers are working now in very difficult circumstances and the expectation on current community development workers is that they will help deliver public services. They are expected to be the ones that have a link between the community and the state and are not to generate lots of activity within communities which gives the state or their employer a headache.'

Tensions: for whose benefit are we working?

> Tensions and dilemmas around the role of community development and how it operates are nothing new to community development practitioners. The recognition of these tensions and how to address them was part of practice for many community development workers during the 1970s and 1980s: Community workers will not succeed unless they are able to live with conflict and tension, as well as being able to recognise and handle problems of power politics. (Calouste Gulbenkian Foundation, 1968, p 76)

What the state wants and what communities want are not necessarily the same, and much of the community development literature refers to the contested nature of community development. What this essentially means is that different political beliefs and positions justify different methods and approaches within community development. Practitioners have tended to work within this tension. Georgina Webster, for example, working during the 1970s and 1980s for Lambeth Council, recognised that the local authority was not a monolith and that different agendas were at play even within the confines of the local authority:

'The council has an agenda and if you are a council employee, you are there to meet that agenda. I was meeting the council's agenda but it was a different bit of the council's agenda to the planning department … helping people to look at what their needs were and how to organise to meet their needs, and that was justified.'

There are always tensions inherent in professional practice within bureaucratic organisations and Georgina Webster's reflection suggests a practitioner thinking politically about her role, aware of the respective agendas at play and how best to support communities within that context. Georgina's approach was not, however, without challenge:

'I had a couple of councillors' complaints because of working on estates with local people to help them get organised to do what they wanted to do. I was employed by social services and the councillors who lived on these estates felt this was inappropriate behaviour so asked questions about my role. I was absolutely supported all the way through by the social services department and explained my professional role to these councillors which was accepted.'

Community development has always faced the dilemma about the extent to which it is managing the incorporation of communities into the work of the state – asking people to participate in their own deprivation. Language used most recently to describe the role of the practitioner talks of social adaptation and changing behaviour (CDF et al, 2006, p 9). In this sense, the state is looking for community development to enable communities to adapt to the new circumstances in which they find themselves, whereby communities are being asked to take greater responsibility for their own problems. Poverty and deprivation become the problems of the poor to which they must find their own answers. In part this bottom–up model underpins a community development approach but a tension exists in terms of what is being expected from communities and what is being avoided by the state.

> 'I don't think that the state listens to ways in which citizens wish to engage. There's a presumption that excluded communities want to get involved and do these things for themselves. We don't hear about credit unions in Tunbridge Wells because they have banks and Lloyds TSB do it all for them. Why should we want to run our own bank? We'd just rather Lloyds TSB come back and do it as they use to before they red-lined this patch.' (David Robinson)

At a community development conference a Home Office civil servant was asked how practitioners and communities could best be heard by civil servants. The response was a stark but honest perspective on the current relationship between community development practice and policy:

> 'Help me meet my targets.'

As in the past, today's practitioners face the tension of meeting policy priorities and community priorities, reflected in the statement above. Whereas in the past, practitioners were able to carve out space to operate, today they struggle to find this room as they are working in a much tighter system of management and accountability invariably funded through government. The tensions are no longer played out in terms of conflicts between practitioners and authorities and can be seen surfacing instead in the interactions between community activists and those representing authority. The role of practitioners has in some sense become one of managing community pressure rather than giving it voice. Many practitioners today articulate fear of such conflict that is intrinsically linked to the insecure and temporary nature of many community development posts. They lack the confidence to challenge and suspect they will not be backed up by their department in the way that Georgina Webster describes above. What does this mean for the interests and wishes of the communities in which they work? How effectively are they being served?

As Paul Henderson describes in Chapter Two, historically, community development has been sponsored by different professions and with each new sponsor has come a new agenda and direction for community development. During the 1970s and into the 1980s the sponsor was that of social work. Ann Chapman recalls "a tension, with the pressure

on community work to become a form of preventative social work
or to fit into community care agendas". Ann and her colleagues were
resistant to these pressures and tried to retain a more generic form of
community work. Their response was to show the ways in which generic
community work helped to build skills and confidence in communities,
and they helped to establish community-based organisations in ways
that were helpful to social work agendas.

John Killion, also working within a context of a social work sponsor,
took a similar route:

> 'We realised that we could do far more if we took a
> more generalist approach, rather than a specific casework
> approach. We actually started looking at what were
> the general problems, things like welfare rights advice,
> developing a strong tenants and residents association on
> the estate, developing a play group which was extremely
> successful.'

While recognised by many as fitting the community development
process most closely, the generic role of community development has
been a major casualty of the change in sponsorship down the decades
as each sponsor has looked for community development to adopt a
more specific role in line with its own interests and concerns. Thus,
the generic neighbourhood worker of the 1970s working to a social
work or anti-poverty agenda is replaced by the community engagement
officer of today, responsible for ensuring that communities are involved
and active within public policy agendas. The few generic posts still in
existence today tend to be funded independently:

> 'The only place I see generic community workers seems to
> be in the faith communities. Churches often still employ
> neighbourhood workers. Unless you have independent
> money to fund community development work, you'll not
> get the generic, creative stuff.' (Greg Smith)

Communities tend not to see the world divided into themes of
regeneration, health, social inclusion and so on. Thus the disappearance
of the generic practitioner impacts on how their needs and wishes
are taken up, or not. It limits the extent to which initiatives aimed at
supporting communities can really understand the issues through the
eyes of those that live the experiences day to day. Similarly, for the

practitioner, the shift to a top-down, sponsor-led agenda challenges core values and processes within community development.

Mark Woodhead provides a graphic picture of how community development, in the context of a regeneration programme in the North West of England during the 1990s, failed to fulfil its potential for either the state or the community:

> 'They came up with this list of community groups in the area and gave it to us and said "we want you to check up on this list, find out how many of these are real groups and how many aren't, make contact with all of them, show us evidence that you've made contact with them and keep that list up to date". It turned into a kind of terror chasing and it felt like we were checking if this is a legitimate and real community group, or is it a front? It deflected us away from what we felt we ought to be doing in terms of building local people's capacity and helping people to engage more effectively in an informed way with the regeneration process.'

With new government initiatives comes the underlying assumption that any one programme is central and that the community is marginal. Rather than working from the needs and wishes of the community, as with the generic approach, the community needs to be fitted in to the programme. Mark Woodhead recognises that how community development is funded is critical to what work takes place, with whom and how. He summarised his experiences during this period as realising that "the person who pays the piper calls the tune".

Managing interests: the values of community development

How do practitioners work effectively within these tensions? For Alan Barr it is about being clear what you are there to do and whether you are able to work effectively:

> 'There is always a dilemma about your relationship between those who employ you and those that you work for. The first thing you've got to do is to set out the parameters within which you're going to be able to work and negotiate those with the people that employ you. If you're put in a position where you would not be free to support people

to present their legitimate concerns, then you shouldn't be working there.'

Alan Barr's reflection mirrors the view of the Gulbenkian Report:

> Community workers often face acute tensions of loyalty to the people they serve. To make people more aware of their needs and more vocal about them may stir up trouble which can lead to expressions more violent than wise. Community workers need great integrity and judgement not to be caught between the cross-fire that results, but on the contrary to help each side to see the other's point of view. If this is not possible, in the last resort the community worker must decide whether he [sic] should either resign or compromise. (Calouste Gulbenkian Foundation, 1968, p 83)

It is interesting that both of the above quotes place emphasis on the responsibility of the practitioner to decide whether or not she/he can work effectively within their place of employment. But what happens when many practitioners across the whole country feel that their values are under threat? Is it still about individual choice or are there wider questions to be asked of the sponsors and employers? Do they bear any responsibility for ensuring that what is preached is practised?

For Gary Craig, the problem lies in part with the nature of the community development profession:

> 'The problem is that too often community development has simply been seen as a skills-based occupation. The BNP uses community work skills to organise its constituency to some degree. So, without a value base and without a theoretical framework, I think the skills fall down, because they can be used anywhere. That has always been one of the tensions of community development because many of the employment opportunities have come in a context where there's been a tension between the values of the organisation and the values of the worker.'

Alan Barr and many other practitioners I have met rely on their values to guide such decisions:

'You have to be clear about your values, be clear about the
principles that underpin the job.'

Presumably, if you are unable to live out your values, this forces you
to evaluate whether you should be working where you are. This is a
personal interpretation of values and their meaning yet the community
development 'profession' also comes with a set of values. Back in the
late 1960s these were articulated in the Gulbenkian Report as being
about humanity and individual potential, participation, diversity and
recognition of the interplay between 'organisation from above and
development from below'. Today the values have been articulated by
CDX as collective working, equality and justice, learning and reflecting,
participation, political awareness and sustainability (CDX, 2006). FCDL
describes additional values of self-determination and reflective practice
(FCDL, 2002). The values of community development as described
in recent statements appear somewhat aspirational with a hope for
equality and justice. Yet, implicit in what Alan Barr says, and what I
have always understood, is that the values of community development
are 'active' and form the basis of our practice. I wonder if articulating
our values as nouns rather than verbs makes it more difficult to apply
the values within practice? Perhaps referring to them as values as
opposed to principles lessens the extent to which they should underpin
community development and can result in the misuse of community
development.

When I began community development in the early 1990s, some of
the community development values that I was made aware of included
the 'empowerment' of individuals and communities, working 'with, not
for' people, seeing community development as a 'bottom-up' process in
which communities define the issues on which we worked for change.
The process, I was told, was as important as the end result.

As I meet with practitioners today, I regularly hear descriptions of
'value conflicts' between the values of the worker and the practice of
the organisation in which she/he is based, whether it be a statutory or
voluntary sector context. The process values at the heart of community
development rub up against the output requirements of funders or the
sponsors' need for communities to develop services and organisations
often before communities themselves are ready. While representing a
widespread sense of conflict, these tensions over interests and control are
not new but are perhaps less openly debated and fought over. Frances
Clarke describes how hard she and others fought to retain their roles
as community development workers:

'We were proper community development workers. We weren't leaders. It's tough not to be the leader and we got into arguments about that but in the end we remembered that our role is to empower other people. When you're taking decisions fast it's often quite hard to do that. It meant it was very strong because the tenants decided. There were meetings on all estates every week. You were the person who did the work that they decided needed doing. You were their legs and they made the decisions.'

Similar conflicts are taking place for community development workers today, but I hear few success stories arising from their struggles for value-led approaches. Perhaps we need to ask whether community development is really able to put these aspirational values into practice. If not, what is the purpose of the value statements – to inspire or to frustrate? If the former, then maybe practitioners and community development organisations need to be increasingly using the values as a negotiating tool to justify community development approaches rather than more output-oriented techniques. Otherwise, there is a danger that the values become just rhetoric, which are dropped in the interests of efficiency and expediency.

Community development approaches

If practitioners draw on the values of community development to manage the tensions and dilemmas they face, how do they then think about the work, and what approach do they adopt to achieve their goals? In the late 1960s, as is the case today, there were different models of community development competing and at times overlapping. We need to place the reflections of those people I have interviewed in the context in which they were practising community development.

The Gulbenkian Report described the role of the community worker as one of identifying social problems and helping to develop solutions – a 'problem-solving process'. It set out four key roles of the worker, continuous throughout the process: defining the problem; setting up structures to promote communication and to facilitate action; setting goals and policies to guide the action; and finally, evaluation of the work carried out. The report described three 'types' of community work: face-to-face work with local groups (neighbourhood work); developing and coordinating services; and national, regional and local planning. Below, I briefly describe these approaches, the practice examples of which will be described in more detail in Chapters Five and Six.

Neighbourhood work

The face-to-face role is more commonly known as neighbourhood work and is detailed clearly in the text by Henderson and Thomas (2002) in which it is described as 'direct face-to-face work with local people who have formed groups or networks to tackle a need or problem they have identified, to give support to each other and/or provide services to people in the area'. Neighbourhood work is geographically defined and is based on the core concepts of social capital, civil society, capacity building and social inclusion. It involves bringing people together to establish community groups and organisations, helping set up these structures, clarifying goals and activity, networking between groups and encouraging dialogue and negotiation with service providers and decision makers. Particular emphasis is placed on relationship building, promoting participation and expanding the 'roles' and 'capabilities' of individuals and the community as a whole. The Gulbenkian Report stresses the tasks of analysis and interpretation that workers must perform and the educational role in which workers enable the community to better understand their problems and what action they may take. Neighbourhood work continues to be practised today in the form of capacity building of community groups and the somewhat scarcer generic practice, although workers are increasingly being encouraged to work across wider areas than just the neighbourhood.

Service coordination

The second role within the Gulbenkian Report regarding the development and coordination of services is principally about processes that bring about changes in the way services operate. This role involves evaluation of services, 'inter-organisational cooperation' (what we now call 'partnership') to provide services, improving communication between service providers and service users and securing new resources. Considerable attention is given to improving communication and joint working across professional areas and organisations. The term 'service coordination' is used rarely nowadays. Previously, it was often used to refer to the work of councils for voluntary service and other umbrella-type organisations.

Social planning

The third area is that of 'social planning' (known today as 'community planning'), and is focused around researching and analysing information to influence planning, whether at a local, regional or national level. It is again based on the recognition that large organisations and authorities can significantly impact on the fortunes of communities and thus need to be influenced by a community development perspective. This role is also very much about working collaboratively with other organisations and core to the role is the job of finding the resources with which to implement the suggested interventions. Community planning is central to current community development practice and underpins the dialogue and partnership models that exist across all areas of practice.

Community action

The Calouste Gulbenkian Foundation set up a Community Work Group in 1970 and three years later published a report that built on the 1968 report. The 1973 report included a chapter on community action, a community development approach which the Community Work Group recognised had gained increasing significance.

The way that the term was used in the UK became distinctive, in comparison with the much wider way that it was used in the US. The thinking of the Community Work Group on community action was influenced by an article written by Richard Bryant. He defined community action as a particular approach to organising local groups and welfare publics: 'an approach in which the political impotence or powerlessness of these groups is defined as a central problem and strategies are employed which seek to mobilise them for the representation and promotion of their collective interests' (Bryant, 1972, p 206). Examples cited included the claimants' and unemployed workers' unions, tenants' associations protesting about rent increases and the squatting movement.

Community action as defined in the 1970s stressed the involvement of those who were poor and deprived, drawing on outsiders who identified with them. The campaigns on housing issues in London's Notting Hill and elsewhere mainly made use of this combination. A national magazine, *Community Action*, was an important source of ideas and support for radical action. The two main characteristics of community action were bargaining and confrontation strategies, the latter often involving rent strikes, demonstrations, sit-ins and other overt expressions of conflict. It was particularly successful in mobilising people when there was a very direct issue about which people felt strongly. Community action was seen as signalling a revival of the social movement origins of community development in contrast to the emergence of the latter as a profession.

Community action lost its high profile in the 1980s and, following the impact of the Thatcher years, the term began to be used in the broader, US sense to refer to a range of community-based activities and actions. Attempts were made by theorists and practitioners to revitalise activities that responded to the needs of the socially and economically oppressed. Today, however, the use of the term in this sense is not widespread.

Community organising

Another approach mentioned by interviewees (but not in the Gulbenkian Report) is that of community organising, a more radical approach originating from the work of Saul Alinsky around the mass organisation of poor people in the US from the 1930s onwards and described in Alinsky's book, *Rules for radicals* (1971). Community organising is about building 'broad based', 'multi–issue' organisations which focus on realistic and common demands – demands that are winnable as opposed to idealistic and demands that are in the self-interest of the organisation's members (Henderson and Salmon, 1995). Key to the approach is the training of professional 'organisers' who build this broad constituency with an understanding and analysis of power that they use to negotiate with the establishment for changes. Community organising is thus about confronting institutions and established organisations, often through negotiation, to bring about change – it is not about providing community-based services or activities.

Community organising has close links with the churches and in the UK it was the *Faith in the city* report (Archbishop's Commission on Urban Priority Areas, 1985) that provided the stimulus for the emergence of community organising. In 1990, Neil Jameson was the organiser behind Communities Organised for a Greater Bristol and is the founder of the Citizens Organising Foundation (COF), based on the community organising model which provides a critique of the neighbourhood-based approach to tackling urban deprivation:

> 'The government is driven by need and problems rather than by talent, by what works. One of the lessons I learnt is that neighbourhood focused initiatives were flawed and are twice as flawed now with globalisation being so prevalent and yet, central government still puts money into pockets of need, whether this be New Deal for Communities or any other such initiative. It hasn't changed since the CDPs and I think in the 21st century, globalisation requires a much more sophisticated response than an area-based, project based, needs-led initiative to social change.' (Neil Jameson)

The increasing centralisation of decision making during the 1980s and 1990s, and the push for practitioners to be working on a government agenda of economic regeneration rather than the expressed needs of local communities, gave rise to an interest in the community organising model. In contrast to what was felt to be the inadequacy of the neighbourhood model to create real change, community organising became a source of hope and inspiration for practitioners who longed to create a link between their aims, values and day-to-day practice.

The Community Development Project

A period of particular interest for community development was that of the national Community Development Project (CDP) (1968-77), which embodied aspects of most of these approaches at different points. CDP was launched by the then Labour government as 'a modest attempt at action research into the better understanding and more comprehensive tackling of social needs, especially in local communities within the older urban areas, through closer co-ordination of central and local official and unofficial effort, informed and stimulated by citizen initiative and involvement' (Home Office, 1971, cited in Lees and Smith, 1975). The purpose was one of tackling poverty and deprivation through cost-effective programmes. Twelve area projects were established in collaboration between central government, local authorities and universities:

> 'The structure within which we were working was quite unique because the central government put up 75% of the money and local government put up 25%. That first of all meant that local government could have it presented to them as essentially £3 for every £1 they spent. That brought some room for manoeuvre. Each team also had a research element which was formally attached to a local university. We then had, if you like, three legs supporting the project.' (Gary Craig)

The history of CDP has been written about at length (CDP Inter-project Editorial Team, 1977), but the crucial point to make here is about the analysis and approach that the CDP adopted. Some, not all, of the CDPs began initially to challenge the government's assumptions on which the programme was based, particularly that the individuals living in deprived areas were themselves the cause of deprivation (social pathology) and thus needed to take an active role in turning things round in their neighbourhoods themselves through self-help activities. A number of the CDPs developed a structural analysis of the issues faced within these deprived areas in which they argued that the causes of deprivation, and thus the potential answers, lay beyond the confines of the 'deprived neighbourhood':

> 'The critical insight of the CDPs was that you had to look way beyond the neighbourhood to understand the causes of urban decline. This is commonplace nowadays, particularly in an era of globalisation, but if you go back 30 years to that period, this was a startling new insight. The message we were trying to convey was that what you might do at a local level might be completely misguided unless you understood the structural context in which you were doing it. Do you simply blind yourself to what's going on around or do you try and situate what's going on within that much broader framework? The very local manifestation of social change needs to be understood as a consequence of decisions that were increasingly being taken by people who had no allegiance to the locality.' (Gary Craig)

As Gary Craig asserts, this analysis was new and directly challenged the policies of government. Through a central information and intelligence unit, CDP began to produce a number of hard-hitting reports that outlined how poverty and deprivation were caused by fundamental inequalities in the economic and political system. In addition, some (not all) of the CDPs began to organise local community groups and tenants' associations and in some cases linked these with industrial struggles, many of which began to use the information and analyses of CDP to criticise council policies around issues such as housing and welfare. CDP began to be viewed as a threat to local and central government and funding was withdrawn from the mid-1970s. The approach of a number of the CDPs had shifted from a model of dialogue with authorities towards a conflict model, as they felt that providing evidence and experiences to policy makers of the reality and causes of poverty and deprivation was failing to result in policy changes.

However, there were other experiences and views within the CDPs than that summarised above. Alan Barr describes his experience of working in Oldham CDP:

> 'It was the last one to start and in some ways it was quite different from the image that people have of the CDP in the sense that those of us who were working there had more of a neighbourhood practice orientation and perhaps were less inclined to be convinced by some of the analysis that

had come out of the earlier CDPs. Not that we didn't think that poverty was structural, but actually we weren't quite sure what we could do about it even if it was.'

As I look around my local area, local manifestations of wider changes include the closure of local hospitals, the loss of local shops, markets and services. These are often what communities are shouting about most loudly yet community development today tends to remain silent on such issues. It is the community organising model or campaigning that picks them up, whereas community planning and neighbourhood work focus on dialogue with service providers. If mainstream practice concentrates on what the government will pay for, such as involvement in community planning structures, is there not a danger that we fail to connect with the reality within communities and the politics from below?

Gary Craig, reflecting back on his experiences of CDP, suggests that since that time, governments have ensured much greater control over community programmes and the activities of community development workers, evidenced by a new level of managerial control from the centre in the form of targets and outputs:

> 'Government learnt the lessons of the CDP. They were never going to let a bunch of radical lunatics loose in community development again. After that, they never created the space for community workers to operate with as much autonomy.'

Current context

In contrast, Alan Barr views the current policy context as much more favourable to the practice of community development than it was in the 1970s:

> 'The policy context for community development now, certainly in Scotland, sets out a framework for the practice of community development which ought to allow you to defend operating within the local state or wherever in a way that involves challenging the way that the state behaves in relation to the communities that you work with and that will be seen as quite legitimate.'

Learning Resources
Centre

All parts of the public sector in Scotland are required to engage communities according to a set of standards which are aimed at ensuring that local people, particularly those who are most disadvantaged, are heard within the planning and delivery of services. In England there is a 'Duty to Involve' on the part of public authorities, introduced within the local government White Paper, *Strong and prosperous communities* (CLG, 2006).

This is a significant change in how the public sector is required to work with communities, particularly when we recall the often patronising and disempowering service that many disadvantaged communities received in the past.

Community development practitioners today, particularly those working within the parameters of government funding, do seem to experience the managerial control that Gary Craig refers to, but perhaps they are unaware what space and influence they may have to defend their practice and challenge the state? The professional climate is one of compliance rather than challenge and practitioners are encouraged neither to think nor to act critically. Delivery has become the mantra for practice and today's practitioners could benefit from the opportunity to think and reflect more, understanding what their role is within bigger processes impacting on communities. Out of this analysis and understanding will come new forms of practice, theory and approaches to community development. The responsibility to kick-start these debates and analysis lies with all of us in the community development field.

Structural analyses and community organising approaches can be found within COF, but in few other UK-based organisations, most likely because of the need to secure independent funding. Far more common for 'mainstream' community development are theories of social capital and civil society that underpin neighbourhood work. Government programmes still pursue very much a neighbourhood-based approach to tackling poverty and deprivation, although suggestions are emerging for practitioners to become more strategic in their work, as in working across whole areas at a policy level rather than within communities with particular groups. Capacity building of community groups to solve their own problems is the dominant form of practice today. Do we need to be clearer just what communities can solve on their own and what involves deeper changes and responsibilities beyond those of the deprived community?

Area-based strategies need to be influenced by a community development perspective if we are serious about change. Community development is provided with an opportunity that will be wasted without an awareness of the tensions and differing interests at play. Community development needs to negotiate and challenge in order to influence rather than remaining silent on policies and practices which conflict with community interests and the values and practice of community development.

Closer links with policy must not result in the removal of practitioners working within communities where support is needed to assist local people to understand, articulate and act on their concerns. It is important that community development does not shift further towards facilitating policy implementation and as a consequence forget the values on which the practice stands.

Training for what?

The role of the community development worker is a challenging one that requires the practitioner to understand theories of change and manage tensions. Such a role suggests the need for a sophisticated level of training and support for workers. Looking back to the 1970s, Jerry Smith feels that this did not exist:

> 'I wasn't very impressed with what I had seen of the community work courses. They tended to be, as higher education was at the time, highly politicised, ramming neo-Marxist messages down everybody's throat. I don't think that was training you to be a community worker and I still don't. I think the quality of community work training in the higher education establishments in the late 1970s and 1980s was absolutely pathetic.'

Is it any better today? Some of the practitioners interviewed questioned whether the focus of much training for community development today is on skills-based competencies embodied within the national occupational standards rather than a deeper understanding of change and how to work with communities to achieve this:

> 'I'm particularly frustrated by some of the approaches that have been taken to training for community work and community development which I think have become trapped in this idea that you can delineate a set of competencies, but actually those competencies only get used in a way that is effective if they're driven by a vision of the kind of change that you're trying to achieve.' (Alan Barr)

'There is an awful lot of people who find themselves in community development rather than having chosen to be in it and they don't necessarily know how to go about it. Lots of community workers that we trained hadn't thought about how to deal with conflict in groups or about communities on the margins and how you bring them in. People are constrained by outputs. There's all these things you've got to deliver that gets in the way of just going with the flow to some extent.' (Mandy Wilson)

The emphasis on skills and competencies stifles reflection, analysis and creativity and has arisen in part as a result of the expansion of community development over the past few years and the focus on community development as a profession. The growth of community development posts has brought in new practitioners who are perhaps less connected to the concept of community development as a process of social change and are more interested in it being a professional career:

'There was a sort of explosion, community development was seen as a way forward and you had all these people employed and the notion that anyone can do community development. They didn't have a skills base, a knowledge base and a value base but they had to be employed, there were jobs there. We never quite got to grips with what community development was at the core.' (Charlie Garratt)

The focus on 'how to' techniques with limited political analysis of what we are trying to achieve, possible approaches, trade-offs and tactical positions one may adopt leaves practitioners ill equipped. Training for community development workers focuses on the technical 'capacity building' and 'engagement' side of the role and has little connection with experiences, theories and aspirations for social change. Either it is a lack of time or interest, but practitioners today are not rushing to read texts on theories of community development and I am not sure how you encourage them to do so. It is hard to understand how practitioners coming into the role today can live up to the aspirations of community development without an awareness of such theories and approaches but perhaps their roles no longer ask this of them?

Nevertheless, for some practitioners, training has never been important:

'I have this kind of feeling that there are people for whom training is irrelevant. I think about the people who I have most regard for in community development. I don't know whether they are trained or not and actually I think it is to do with the kind of people they are and just their understanding of what makes groups tick.' (Alan Barr)

The growing importance of the role of activists and volunteers within communities may provide community development with a pool of workers who, based on their lived experiences, have the connection to social change and how individuals and groups 'tick' that Alan Barr refers to. In this scenario, training may need to become less focused around the 'training course' and qualifications which practitioners often are not interested in and more about 'on-the-job' learning to enable them to effect change:

'One characteristic which cuts across some of the rather prissy ideas about development work is that you "learn by doing". We discovered this way back and nothing has ever happened to tell me to change.' (Mel Witherden)

The *Survey of community development workers* (Glen et al, 2004) highlighted that there are individuals within communities who have been active in community development projects for many years and have begun to acquire the skills that are often seen as the domain of professional workers. These individuals tend to be highly committed to their communities and have a particular understanding of how things work on the ground. The study points to the need for 'less formal', 'accessible, localised' training, which is relevant and sensitive to the education experiences of the individuals participating. Thus, the role of these activists presents professional community development and community development training with an interesting but timely challenge to produce literature, training and support that enables activists to promote social change with and for communities.

Community development is at a critical point – reflected in the title of a joint CDX and Scottish Community Development Network conference, 'Everywhere and Nowhere', held in Edinburgh in 2006. Professional community development is more closely linked to policy than ever before. This brings with it the hope of influence but also the fear that aims, values and community interests are fading away behind policy priorities and funding targets.

Practitioners tend to perceive the problems that communities face as located in reasons deeper than the failure of communities themselves. Nevertheless, this understanding does not marry up with practice which leans more to a social pathology model in areas of high deprivation: helping communities to tackle their own problems with no connection to the wider causes of the decline and deprivation in which they live. Nor does training for practitioners always promote a vision of change and a deeper level of analysis, focusing instead on the technical competencies that are required to develop community-based organisations.

If the community development profession is serious about the goals of equality and justice that it espouses then it needs to establish a connection between aims, values and practice. Reflection and critical thinking within the field of community development is needed to produce new opportunities for practice which connect more closely with issues of poverty and justice and enable practitioners to challenge as well as compromise.

FIVE

Achieving change: the rise of partnerships and their impact on community development practice

What did practitioners used to do? How did they work and what approaches did they adopt? We have described the changing context for community development practice since the 1970s and discussed different perspectives on roles, values and approaches to community development. In this chapter we will be looking at the way practitioners worked by drawing on the examples provided by interviewees. These are intended to flesh out earlier discussions. The chapter will look in turn at community development inspired by conflict approaches, followed by the more recent shift towards a community planning model based on dialogue and partnership working.

Community development as a vehicle for community demands

As described in earlier chapters, the 1970s and early 1980s witnessed a variety of approaches to community development. It appears that some models of community development were considerably more challenging of the state than community development practice today. Practitioners who took this more challenging approach understood that one of their key roles was to support local communities to challenge and make demands on the local state based on their needs and wants. Challenges and conflicts were seen to be inevitable aspects of good community development:

> 'If communities are being properly and effectively supported by a community worker, those communities will very often challenge the way in which they [authorities] are trying to manage their area.' (Dean Huggins)

Community development was seen as a process for uniting communities around common grievances such as the condition of housing or the lack of local services. The process of change that defines community development would be achieved through making demands on the local state and challenging authority. It is not that individuals and communities never complained without the presence of community workers, but with the input of paid workers, those demands became more coordinated and directed. Individual complaints did not pose a threat to the policies and practices of a local authority but a campaign for better housing involving hundreds of residents took on a different meaning and complexion for decision makers and elected representatives. Working in this way, practitioners were often closely aligned with the communities in which they worked. Many were seen as 'trouble makers' by the authorities and agencies that employed them.

This conflictual approach within practice was exemplified in workers adopting a campaigning style, supporting local communities to lobby and pressurise authorities. Workers would identify what were initially seen as private, individual issues and bring people together to enable them to realise the collective nature of the issues they faced. Welfare benefits and advice issues lent well to such an approach:

> 'People would say, "Well, what's the role of a community worker?" and for me it's about turning individual issues into collective issues. We ran a welfare benefits campaign, drawing in the religious centres from the Sikh and Muslim communities. We knew you can't run a campaign without there being somebody to pick up the enquiries and so we set up a welfare benefits advice surgery. Almost overnight the flow of people from the Asian and African–Caribbean communities into that area office just rocketed and suddenly they were the majority user. My focus was the collective community-wide response.' (Gersh Subhra)

Recalling her work in Lambeth during the mid-1970s, Georgina Webster recognised that bringing the community together to make such demands was much easier when the community had got nothing to lose and the "enemy" was very obvious. In the communities with which Georgina Webster worked, many of them were living in awful accommodation and they were not prepared to simply survive. These were politically charged times in which conflict and challenge were seen as the most effective route to get what you wanted. While many communities today continue to live in poverty and deprivation, the political climate does not encourage communities to adopt such a stance. Talk of 'enemies' was very much linked to the organising language of Saul Alinsky, and indicated how some practitioners saw there to be clear sides within a conflict in which their role was to support the community to achieve victory.

'Enemies' could also be allies. Frances Clarke, working in Community Links in East London from the late 1970s, remembers how they built support for their campaign activities:

> 'We were good at building partnerships as community workers. We would never accept we had an enemy. Nobody was an enemy. Everybody is a potential partner. You expect more of people if you put them under pressure.' (Frances Clarke)

Frances' point is enormously significant for the current context in which we find ourselves. Arguably, the approach of creating partners rather than 'enemies' is what we have witnessed since the mid to late 1980s. However, Frances' reflection also implies something more about power and control. Her organisation, Community Links, had a clear aim and agenda, making partners of those that might seem unlikely bedfellows but in the process, putting them under pressure to make things happen. The approach to change that is suggested by this example is one of influence and pressure in which the community development organisation and practitioners are influencing others to achieve the community's aim. Does the current context of partnerships, rooted in collaborative working across sectors, encourage this type of independence and influence on the part of communities and community organisations? Practitioners and community organisations often describe themselves as being controlled by the partnership and its agenda and can, ironically, feel disempowered through such arrangements.

In the past, practitioners did not simply start working in a community and immediately begin supporting the disparate demands being put forward. The role of the worker was an educational one in which she/he assisted communities to understand the problems they faced and why they were happening. The worker then provided support to develop appropriate demands. Working in the Benwell area of Newcastle during the mid-1970s, Gary Craig took part in a campaign to confront the hostility of some local people towards the increasing arrival of Indian and Pakistani landlords into the area who were buying up property and letting them out to students. He recounts how he went about the issue:

'Now, what's the demand that you might make about Indian landlords coming in and buying up houses. Do you go to the council and say "stop Indian landlords buying houses"? Well, politically and ideologically that's unacceptable. It's unworkable because it's a housing market and people will buy. But if you get people to understand that there is a severe housing shortage in terms of cheap accommodation for students, where do you start directing your demands? Local people then need to start thinking about what the appropriate demands are and who they direct them to. Nobody had really thought about the fact that it was the university that they ought to be taking it to.' (Gary Craig)

Students were not looking after the rented properties resulting in a decline in the quality of housing and the wider neighbourhood. Asian landlords were part of a wider process, not the cause of the problem. Rather than simply targeting Asian landlords, the issues became about regulating landlords, regulating numbers of people in flats, controlling rents and regulating noise. The result was that discussions were held with the university to improve its accommodation policy. Tenants groups also met with student representatives to express their needs. Gary Craig reflects that his role in this example was about:

'... making sense of processes in the neighbourhood which sometimes people are not equipped with because of education or knowledge or contacts or simply because they don't have time. They are not equipped to understand actually what's going on. All over the area there was a process of decline which manifested itself in all sorts of ways.'

The education role of the community development practitioner has waned over the years, particularly with the move away from generic practice towards more specialised roles. It is key to enabling communities to understand the factors that impact on their lives and is a core element underpinning the values of empowerment and self-determination within community development (see Freire, 2000; Ledwith, 2006). Helping communities to 'make sense' of processes and understand problems has fallen away as the emphasis on targets and delivery has increased. The government's community cohesion agenda provides perhaps the only opportunity for practitioners and communities to engage in this type of analysis and reflection so as to arrive at an understanding of why community conflicts arise and how these might be prevented. This is because the cohesion agenda acknowledges the need for community dialogue and debate and makes space and time for these types of activities. The government appears to understand that cohesion cannot be imposed on communities and thus needs communities themselves to understand and engage meaningfully within these discussions (CLG, 2008).

Campaigning community work in the 1970s often had a real sense of purpose and energy which was why local people got involved in large numbers. Campaigns involved a great deal of groundwork in local communities through which trust and relationships were established. Mandy Wilson worked in Newham during the late 1970s and 1980s as part of the Newham Tower Blocks Campaign:

> 'Every day we were leafleting tower blocks, getting people to come out and talk to us. We used to take the double-decker bus, park it in the middle of the estate and I used to go round with a loudhailer shouting "come down". We ran some social activities that took a long time to get going. On one of them, for example, we ran a drop-in and a food co-op and we started to get people coming in who lived in the block who didn't know each other, hated each other. We started to bring people together a bit and to do things that brought out their strengths and they started to have some respect for each other.'

Mandy and her colleagues in the campaign got to know people on the estates and were able then to harness their energy and enthusiasm and get them campaigning. They were successful in opening up previously disused community rooms within the tower blocks where many of these activities could take place. But, this was only part of the story:

> 'At the same time we were constantly on the council's back about issues like cockroaches. We used to run "cockroach days" where people brought their cockroaches out of their flats and put them in jars and we took them up to the Housing Department. We did work on dampness, asbestos in blocks, and a lot around children and play in blocks. We were doing all that as well as going to every housing committee meeting so that we could feed back to tenants on what was happening.' (Mandy Wilson)

Other practitioners were involved in supporting campaigns through carrying out research, digging up facts for the campaign, advising campaign members on how to make use of the information, providing contacts and advising on planning and strategies. A particular tactic within campaigning community work was to monitor the workings of the authorities and, where possible, put officials under pressure. This ranged from groups of local volunteers reading all the council minutes and reports to find out what was going on through to attending council meetings to make sure officials knew they were being observed:

> 'If people want to influence decisions, they've got to understand how they are made. We were overtly political. We put councillors under such pressure. We used the media to put councillors under pressure and then physically put them under pressure. So we would force our way into the council chamber and you'd be sitting next to councillors who were trying to make decisions and they'd be being filmed on the BBC at the same time. It was very politicising for the tenants.' (Frances Clarke)

These examples provide an insight into the tactics and methods used within practice at this time. Many of the campaigns contained highly creative work designed to raise the profile of groups and influence opinion and decisions. A significant number of practitioners were political in their approach, working with a clear sense of injustice and inequalities that created an urgency within many of the campaigns. Gersh Subhra, working in Derby, had this to say:

> 'I think that we were lucky in the 1980s and before where things were so sharply focused: the miner's strike, poll tax, immigration issues, the National Front. Those sorts of issues were so in your face that you couldn't help but be politicised. It felt like a much easier time to be politicised.'

Once appropriate demands were formed, it was invariably to the senior council officers or councillors in the area that they were directed. While in many cases the submission of community demands resulted in conflict, this was not always the case as some officers and members saw pressure as necessary for change:

> 'He [the director of Housing] always used to give me a telling off and he'd say, "I want you to have those tenant

groups banging on my door and causing trouble because that's the way things ought to be. I need to know what their concerns are. You ought to be generating that kind of activity". That thinking is not around now.' (Charlie Garratt)

This sense of the need for pressure on officers also applied to some councillors where pressure from the community on the councillor would in some cases result in more money being invested in the area:

'The more we were generating demands and needs, the more money was actually coming into his [councillor] neighbourhood and of course that would be a payback because he could present himself then as the "man of the people". Although publicly he may have been angry that people are dumping rats on the Town Hall steps, privately, he might be thinking, "it's an extra £100,000 investment in housing or a better bus service". It's the classic thing about representative democracy needing an active participative democracy to breathe life into it.' (Gary Craig)

Conflict therefore had potential benefits for the councillor, the council officer and the community and was recognised as part of the change process. Today, conflict is very much avoided and practitioners are often employed to manage conflict rather than providing it with an outlet. Partnerships and dialogue have replaced the model of conflict; the pressure that was once exerted by practitioners and communities has in part been replaced by managerial pressures through performance management targets and outputs. Perhaps it is assumed that these managerial pressures mirror the community pressures described above, yet they often reflect policy concerns and agendas rather than community concerns. What is more, a growing number of voluntary organisations have increasingly become part of the bureaucracy, contracted to deliver services for communities.

While conflict had benefits, it also had its drawbacks. The energy, commitment and creativity within many community development projects were often accompanied by arguments and factions, in some cases resulting in the closure of projects. Practitioners describe ideological splits within some organisations that were hotly debated, sometimes to the detriment of work within communities. In these situations conflicts got in the way of progress and workers found it difficult to work with those who did not see the world from their perspective.

Creating space

Today, practitioners do not have the freedom and autonomy to be involved in campaigns and pressure group activities. This space did not always exist either for practitioners in the 1970s and 1980s and had to be fought for. Working in Oldham, Alan Barr and his colleagues were challenging council assumptions as to whether local communities had a right to influence what happened to them. While based within the borough solicitors office within the council, the team took the decision to mount a public inquiry on a compulsory purchase order on local housing together with a local community organisation. Told by the department that they would face the sack if they continued, Alan and his colleagues ignored the warning and proceeded with the campaign:

> 'We decided that you can either do community work from a principled stance, or you didn't do it at all. So we fought the public inquiry and won. We, meaning the local community organisation, fought the inquiry but with our support. It was rather difficult then for our employer to say "hang on, what you've been doing isn't legitimate" and that then created space for us. It made them think in a different way and was a very interesting dialogue.'

Through making a principled stance, Alan Barr and his colleagues were able to defend their work with communities within Oldham and defend the interests of those communities. Of particular interest was the positive impact the conflict had on relationships between the community work team and other officers within the council who viewed the team and its role in a new light, resulting in a shift from confrontation to dialogue.

Other practitioners, especially those based in local authorities, tried to create space through delivering enough of the 'acceptable' work – playgroups and pensioners' clubs, for example – which built credibility and support with councillors and senior officers. This allowed them greater freedom to engage in more controversial activities. In Community Links, David Robinson describes a similar balancing act:

'The advantage of an organisation like Community Links doing different things is that some of those things might be soft social care activities which nobody could really object to while at the same time, under cover of those activities, we could be doing some things which are a bit more controversial perhaps. I just say that on the basis that we earn our mandate from the social care type activities and through that we collect evidence that we have a responsibility to share.'

While there are practitioners today, particularly those working in a local government or partnership setting, who adopt similar approaches to give themselves space, this may be a disappearing art within community development.

In terms of approaches based on pressure and conflict, they have been somewhat overshadowed in mainstream community development today by the move towards a more collaborative way of working across professional disciplines and boundaries in the form of partnerships. Campaigning community development is still practised but tends to be found within the more radical social change and political movements such as anti-deportation and anti-racist campaigns that sit outside the professional community development world.

From conflict to dialogue

Having worked on campaigns and lobbying activities during the 1970s and early 1980s, some practitioners began to question the effectiveness of the conflict model in achieving the aims advanced by community campaigns. This was at a time when local authorities, under threat from the Conservative government, were showing greater interest in working with the voluntary sector to achieve their aims. Local authorities were establishing community development departments in their own right to take forward work with communities. Practitioners began to realise that other strategies were possible and might even work better. The concept of partnerships began to emerge and practitioners wondered if change was more likely to be achieved through dialogue with decision makers rather than simply presenting them with demands. David Robinson describes the shift in approach within Community Links:

'We would try to bring answers rather than shout about problems. Government or the local authority may not agree with our answer but our opening position is: here's an answer and this is the problem that it was an answer to. Maybe what we were doing before was waving the placards about a problem rather than being positive and constructive in our solution. Obviously that then leads to some process about negotiation and bartering where your answer may not be the answer they're prepared to pay for, but already the conversation has moved on to different kinds of answers rather than whether or not there's a problem.'

The idea of providing solutions rather than just problems has been evident within the practice of community development workers for many years. Community development often involved working with communities to develop services and activities where none existed before, generating new and sometimes innovative provision within communities. John Killion describes such an example from his work in Rochdale during the early 1980s:

> 'We discovered that we had a number of children in the area who had fairly severe educational and physical needs and so we looked at what provision was there for them in the school holidays, and there was none at all throughout the whole of Rochdale – nothing. We initially looked at taking over one of the special schools for four weeks in the summer and employing some of the specialist teachers. We also recruited volunteer 5th and 6th formers who the teachers and other specialist nurses and playworkers trained. We borrowed underused school and care establishment minibuses and recruited other volunteers to drive them. In the first year we just ran one summer scheme but that expanded to schemes in every holiday and on most weekends. In some cases, this was the first time these young people had engaged with people from their local community, having been bussed to and from special school, hospital, and respite care. This had a great affect on the kids themselves but it also was of tremendous benefit to other users of the playschemes who gained real positive experiences of being and working with people with disabilities. However, perhaps the greatest effect was on other family members who got respite from constant care needs.'

Many practitioners were working during the 1980s to enable disadvantaged communities to gain access to services and resources that would tackle the inequalities communities experienced. Gaining access meant working with the providers of services, and adopting a conflictual stance was not felt to be the most effective approach. Gersh Subhra was working with black and minority ethnic communities in Derby at the time:

> 'The theme of those early pieces of work relate to working with communities on the one hand and with service providers on the other, who were predominantly white and who were reaching predominantly white communities. We were trying to bring communities together with providers to ask how we can ensure a dialogue that widens access that enables you to reach communities that feel they are not being reached. The idea of trying to drive a wedge into the doors of predominantly white mainstream service providers and to take the community with us in that dialogue was certainly a strong theme of that early work.'

Through engaging with service providers and local authorities from the outset and understanding their context and agendas, relationships and trust would be built and a dialogue for change established. Through this dialogue, providers would better understand the needs of communities and be more responsive in how they acted:

> 'We discovered that when you get people in communities together with people that provide services and they start to see why it is [that] people are concerned about particular issues, you get quite a sympathetic response.' (Alan Barr)

Decision makers and service providers are also interested in influencing the attitudes and behaviour of communities, whether towards education or health or in their willingness to be active in their communities. Mel Witherden, a practitioner in Wales since the early 1970s, articulates the difficulty for a practitioner in this situation:

> 'I wonder what it actually means to "develop that community" because the only way you get them to change the way they regard education, unemployment, ill health, is to tell them that they've got something which is rubbish already, that they shouldn't actually like living there and they should probably find a different way of leading their

life. I think that is a challenge to community development, as to what you do in that situation.'

Practising as a neighbourhood community development worker in inner-city Leeds for 13 years, Tony Herrmann recalls the shift from what he describes as "patronised council estate tenants" who were recipients of services to residents becoming involved in associations and committees in which they began to manage the estate. The level of resident involvement that Tony developed on a large council estate was the result of a long-term strategy of community organisation building and the development of representative structures at a community level. From the initial development of local community groups grew patch-based tenants' associations and ultimately an estate management board on which community representatives from the different areas of the estate were represented. In the process, residents began to meet with officers from the council and to hold them accountable. Tony recalls how residents challenged officers from the highways department about how they were getting a worse deal on average than other areas in Leeds:

> '"This is the pothole outside my house, it has not been repaired for three years. What is your budget for that? What are you doing about it?" It is a very powerful process because nobody had ever called those sorts of services to account before in that kind of way. Some of them responded positively and said, "you know, you're right. We're not spending enough, so we've worked out that this is what the average should be and we've increased it by whatever, 50% or something. So, there's the budget for next year, it's gone up. What do you want us to spend it on?"'

As well as enabling residents to meet with council officers and make them aware of the reality within the local neighbourhood, the development of community-based structures enabled residents to better engage with councillors:

> 'What the councillors saw was a transformation from a mass of individuals who came to their surgeries with problems, a mass of people who were just angry, fed up, alienated and hated living there, into a positive structure where people were organised and started to understand how decisions were made, what budgets were and how

they could negotiate. They thought it was wonderful.' (Tony Herrmann)

In fact, Tony Herrmann's work in this area of Leeds culminated in the establishment of the Belle Isle Foundation, an umbrella body made up of the different community groups in the area which had an education focus and operated along the lines of a development trust (before development trusts were more widely known). The Foundation was able to negotiate with schools, colleges, universities, the local council and with residents in order to embed learning and skills development on the estate:

> 'I saw the Foundation in some ways as a very positive end result of community organisation building, of having various organisations geographically based, linked under this banner of the Foundation and creating a sustainable base for carrying on.' (Tony Herrmann)

In terms of the shift from campaigning to dialogue, Charlie Garratt makes an interesting point about how the community organisation building that he was involved with in the housing field structured and formalised community activity, creating organisations that became more accountable and bureaucratic, which could try to influence but not campaign:

> 'Nobody talks about tenants' groups these days, everybody talks about tenants' associations and the thinking was that somehow you had to structure all of them. If the local authority was to have a relationship with a tenants' group, it had to be formally constituted, it had to be accountable, it had to have a constitution, a chair, a secretary, a formalising of that relationship. Community development workers would help form those constitutions and support that process, but once you have that formal constitution it has to become an association, it has to become something which is a bit of the bureaucracy. It's not up against the barricades fighting and campaigning, it's there as an influencing tool and not as a lobbying or campaigning tool.'

This description of the formalisation of community activity and community interests shows how having a seat at a formal table can often come at the cost of the group losing its freedom to campaign and lobby.

The bureaucracy surrounding community activity can be viewed as a way of enabling people to participate within state planning structures or, alternatively, as a way of stifling dissent and protest from communities through focusing on the rules and avoiding the issues being raised. The concept of capacity building today is similarly viewed by some practitioners as technical community development stripped of its politics and agenda for social justice. From this perspective, community development ignores how problems are experienced by communities, the causes of these problems and what power communities have to influence them – the 'why' of community development. Instead, attention and energy is focused on organisational development and the mechanisms and needs of authorities and partnerships through which it is assumed change will be achieved with limited struggle.

An enduring aspect of many community development workers' role has been the need to work effectively with local councillors. Paramjit Oberoi, working in Derby and Nottingham, recognised this aspect of her practice as a key to achieving change:

> 'I learnt that the way in which sustained progress is going to happen is to work with councillors to help them understand what you're doing and that takes time. It doesn't happen overnight and when you try and get things through council very quickly or just to get the nod, they won't be sustained.'

The need for collaborative work between communities, community organisations and councillors is a topical issue today with the drive to devolve services to the neighbourhood level and councillors described as performing a community leadership role. Working in partnership in this way contrasts with the idea that councillors and council officers need pressure from the community to give the arguments of the latter greater weight. Why don't we need the pressure on authority that practitioners such as Frances Clarke and Charlie Garratt described as necessary in earlier periods? Is it because the officials and the structures are now much more receptive to community needs and wishes? Or is it because we lack the confidence to pressurise and raise our voices about such issues for fear that any gains made might be lost?

From dialogue to negotiation

The partnership model is not a magic wand that waves away all the tensions that have existed previously between community and state interests, particularly around which of these has most control. It is assumed that those participating will have a positive experience. This, however, has not proved to be the case to date. Differentials in power continue to exist within partnership structures with community representatives often isolated and lacking the clout that others bring to the table. Alan Barr recognises these power differentials:

> 'I learnt that you need to enter into that kind of dialogue with service providers from a position of strength … community organisations need to know what they want to achieve, they need to have established the strength of purpose to carry something through over a long period which may require quite frustrating negotiations. They need to look at short-term gains and long-term gains and they need to have a mixture of goals so they can see progress is being made.'

It seems, then, that negotiation rather than dialogue is the important theme to hang on to for both communities and practitioners involved in partnerships and planning structures. In order to negotiate effectively, communities and their representatives need to know where they stand and have a good understanding of what can be won and lost:

> 'The key lesson is analysing what's going on. What kind of relationship have we got here? How secure is it? What are the boundaries within which it can operate? What are the limits of the influence that it can have? Beyond those points, what would the consequences be and at what point would you say those consequences are such that we need to either pull out of this partnership or take a different stance in relation to it which is more challenging?' (Alan Barr)

In theory, challenge and even conflict may still occur within the partnership model but whether this happens in practice is a different matter. Community representatives can feel isolated and shut out if they attempt to challenge or criticise those with power, and the structures themselves guard against such criticism while describing the need for honest dialogue. Bob Holman's extensive experience of neighbourhood work has taught him that it is sometimes difficult for those in local community groups to be angry or critical as they may lose funding, support or the cooperation they need from those with power. He sums up the need for these community groups to be "as wise as doves in their work". How can communities both participate within these structures and also negotiate effectively? What is preventing practitioners from challenging, when necessary, as described in Alan Barr's example from his work in Oldham? How do we ensure that core principles are at the heart of an appropriate stance, as Alan suggests? Clearly, communities, with the support of practitioners, need to be in a position of strength but for many practitioners and community representatives this higher ground is hard to reach.

Local authorities are now required to engage with communities around the planning and delivery of services and therefore communities at last have a seat at the decision-making table from which they were previously excluded. However, this elevated position has not been used to its full potential. In part this is because communities and representatives are unclear how to operate and negotiate effectively, but it is also because of the characteristics of the partnerships themselves. The processes, structures and language of partnerships tend to attract a limited range of similar people, often with bureaucratic skills. Marilyn Taylor (2003) has highlighted the heavy expectations that are placed on community representatives to act as a bridge between statutory structures and deprived and disadvantaged communities, which can easily result in unrealistic workloads and subsequent burn-out, and this was recently confirmed by work carried out by the Community Development Foundation (CDF) during 2006. Some community representatives become pulled between their community and the partnership and can lose credibility in the eyes of the community if they come to identify too closely with the partnership. Is involvement in such structures becoming an end in itself rather than focusing on the changes that communities wish to happen? Can community development workers play a key role in enabling community organisations and community representatives to maximise their influence and impact in such contexts to create the desired changes?

Interestingly, the community planning approach described in Chapter Four makes reference to the concept of negotiation, a tactic which is central to the community organising model summarised in the same chapter. Community organising is sceptical that social change for the disadvantaged ever occurs through top-down structures or government initiatives and believes that what is needed is for community organisations to come together to negotiate with these structures from a position of strength. On the surface the language of negotiation, using strength often based on an analysis of power, is similar to language used by those advocating the community planning model. There the similarity ends as the community organising model uses its analysis to negotiate rather than participate within existing structures and partnerships. The approach that practitioners of this model take is to analyse the different agendas round the table and to pressurise and advocate based on the interests of the community, not to attend and participate within the structures and agenda laid out by the partnership. Thus, it is a very different approach to that of helping communities participate more effectively in the existing partnership structures.

> 'As a community worker, I don't think I ever talked about power, I always talked about "when is the next action" ... we never actually did an analysis of how much power have we got and how much power have they got and pragmatically, what business can we do together. Once you get into the language of power, you begin to think of negotiation as a strategy rather than demonstration, but you can't negotiate if you can't get round the table.' (Neil Jameson)

Working within Community Links, David Robinson has seen government become more responsive to the work of his organisation and knows that Community Links is listened to more than ever before. David has learnt, however, that for change to actually happen, just being heard is not enough:

> 'Being given the opportunity to speak is different to being heard and acted upon and even if you have the opportunity to make the case at a very senior level, at ministerial level, you think, "that's it, we've cracked it now, we've got this opportunity to make this point to the Chancellor". The real responsibility for following through what we talk about, no matter how enthusiastic he was, is with those grade 7 civil servants who never thought it was a good idea in the first place, and actually change is about influencing people at a whole series of points in the process.'

Dialogue through partnerships and community planning has become the defining model for community development practice today. While it appears to bring significant gains in terms of more responsive and accountable public services, it has consistently failed to support bottom-up, community-led action that is independent of government priorities and based on what communities may wish to happen. Meaningful dialogue rests on the need for trust, honesty and the ability to disagree, but questions remain as to whether communities and practitioners can really challenge with confidence within existing structures. The community planning model is a pragmatic approach to change based on developing relationships, influencing perceptions and ultimately decisions. It challenges what some may see as the idealistic wish for self-determination and suggests that maybe a little bit of influence and control is better than none at all. But does community engagement in community, neighbourhood and area forums really influence the decisions and priorities at the higher levels of strategic decision making? While existing structures can provide for some things, are they really enough to allow for significant improvements in the health and wealth of more deprived communities?

Working 'strategically'

Before we conclude, a short note about the strategic nature of community development that is essential if communities and practitioners are to hold out hope of achieving the changes that they put forward as priorities. Different people mean different things when using the term 'strategic'. Mandy Wilson describes how, during the Newham Tower Blocks Campaign, working strategically meant being clear about her aims in the context of multiple needs but limited resources:

> 'There was one community worker employed by the council and that was it, so I had to be quite strategic. I was a community worker across the whole borough so I had to think about what it is we're trying to achieve here and initially we said, "we're trying to bring people together living in the blocks that were isolated".' (Mandy Wilson)

Mandy Wilson was able to work strategically, using her time wisely to achieve the goals of the campaign. Today, for practitioners employed by statutory authorities, 'strategic' often relates to how practitioners assist the realisation of the strategic goals of the authority. In fact, current trends in community development suggest that practitioners are gradually moving towards more area-based policy roles – in order to meet 'strategic' priorities – and away from work at the grass roots. This raises concerns as to how workers will be informed by community perspectives to, in turn, influence agendas. If these positions are about policy implementation in communities then they offer little opportunity for community empowerment; but if recast as roles to influence the direction and priorities of authorities, then they become an opportunity for community influence.

It is worth noting that community development strategies in the context of local authorities started to emerge from the early 1990s and have been used since as a way of planning where and how to use the resources of community development across an authority. The strategies enable the authority to step back and assess the different community needs and interests across an area and adopt what Alan Barr describes as a 'rational analysis' as to how these needs can be prioritised and met with available resources, rather than have planning based on the subjective expression of individual communities. These strategies have developed a greater prominence as they now feed into the overall community strategy for an area and in turn link to major government funding streams.

To plan effectively and thus work strategically it is vital that you know your area and what is going on. At one level this is about understanding the communities in which you work and having the facts at your fingertips. It also means knowing who is around you in terms of other organisations and who works where within the authorities and partnerships. As Mandy Wilson describes below, networking of a political nature was essential to achieving change:

> 'Networking was one thing that I did a lot of at that time.
> There was a conscious strategy that in order to be able to
> make any changes in Newham you had to network with
> a lot of other people. Nobody came and said to me "oh,
> there's a National Housing Liaison Committee, do come".
> I consciously found those things.'

This issue of networking between practitioners and other professionals and agencies is gaining increasing prominence with the government's drive to get authorities and the voluntary and community sector to work together better. Practitioners will thus be encouraged to make these links through the push to improve and localise service delivery that may also reduce the isolation and fragmentation of community development workers.

As described by practitioners earlier in this chapter, practice in the 1970s and 1980s involved working on the one hand with communities, and on the other with the decision makers within authorities to challenge and influence their thinking. In order to network and influence effectively, awareness and understanding of the policy context was vital. Jerry Smith suggests that perhaps this is harder these days with the plethora of government initiatives and programmes:

'There were far fewer initiatives around in those days so there was less to get your head round than there is now. But such as there were, we did have our heads pretty well round them and we could see their importance and relevance to our work. Whether we did or didn't like them we could see that they were important and we had to take them into account.'

Many practitioners in the 1970s and 1980s would make sure that they attended council meetings, scrutinising the minutes and reports so that they understood exactly what was happening. The complaint from practitioners today is that there just is not the time to do all this as well as deliver the outputs they are expected to achieve. They are certainly less free to pursue their own strategies and are overloaded with tasks in ways their predecessors were not. Is a possible reason for a lack of 'strategic' thinking and practice on the part of practitioners a loss of focus on social change? If that is the case then practitioners have lost the reason to understand the context, scrutinise policy and network politically. Within the partnership model, communities, community organisations, practitioners and those representing the field of community development need to start to challenge more and push the boundaries of what can and cannot be said and done. We need to widen the space within which we practise and, expecting the compromises, be bold in our decisions and approach.

SIX

Who is it for? Accountability and community development

The community development approach has and continues to be influenced enormously by the increased accountability required of practitioners and the community development field as a whole. Discussion and debate around the need for evidence is now a staple ingredient of any community development conference. This chapter will look at how the issues of evaluation, evidence and accountability were addressed in the past through the experiences of practitioners and what this meant for practice. These experiences will be used to make sense of the rising demands for accountability on the work of practitioners today and the implications this has for the type of relationships developed between practitioners and communities. Twinned with this shift towards greater accountability has been an emphasis on partnerships, as outlined in earlier chapters. Communities and the voluntary and community sector are being asked to participate and 'deliver' in more ways than ever before. What does this mean for community development practice? To what extent does it need to adapt its methods and skills?

Evaluation and evidence

In its early days, community development was subject to very little in the way of reporting requirements to those bodies that funded the work. Employing organisations as well as practitioners were afforded a considerable degree of freedom in defining the purpose and processes for their work, allowing them to be responsive to the communities in which they worked. The downward pressures on practitioners that define life in the public and voluntary sectors today had not hit in quite the same way in the 1970s and early 1980s:

> 'A sense of measuring, evaluating or recording anything that you were doing was just minimal. There was no pressure from local authorities to come up with anything, no pressure from managers and not a lot of pressure from the funders

that were putting in the money. That environment just wasn't there.' (Gersh Subhra)

This is not to suggest that without these upward reporting requirements practitioners were necessarily unclear what they were doing or what was expected of them. While the language of outcomes was not used in the mid-1970s, Alan Barr suggests that this is what he has always been working towards:

> 'I was quite clear that what I was looking for were outcomes that would have tangible benefits that people themselves would recognise.'

Perhaps it is possible for practitioners to identify and work towards outcomes that resonate for communities without the need for top-down structures that prescribe outcomes, thus skewing the process of community development?

A perceived gap in stringent measurement and evaluation within the wider public sector came under attack from the Conservative government of the 1980s that used the lack of a performance culture to attack public services and highlight the supposed benefits of privatisation. New Labour opened up a dimension of this 'mind set' when it launched a high profile commitment to reform public services and introduce what is sometimes referred to as 'new managerialism'. Thus, along with all areas of the public sector, community development has become increasingly required to account for its activity. Targets, outputs, indicators and outcomes form the language of new managerialism and are being applied to the aims and activities of community development. While there have been significant challenges for community development (as well as other areas of the public sector) with the introduction of this approach, it must also be acknowledged that some community development practitioners saw the need for much greater accountability:

> 'It was overdue that we needed to evidence what we were achieving in community development. Far too much was taken on trust. We do need to measure success but it's not about things like the number of jobs you've created or the number of houses renovated because the things that it's about aren't easily measurable. It's essentially about confidence building and empowerment and communities being able to achieve things for themselves. It's all about

having a target, having something you want to achieve and being able to show six months later that you've achieved it.' (Jerry Smith)

The process of community development discussed in Chapter Four, in which practitioners develop relationships within communities, identify common concerns and support communities to take collective action, does not happen overnight. It is a gradual process that requires time, energy and a commitment to ongoing resourcing. Furthermore, the process is founded on the principle that communities define for themselves what their problems are and what needs to be done about them. Here is the tension. Contrary to media stereotypes, deprived communities have often been active over many years, explaining at meetings what their problems are and how these can be addressed. Nevertheless, the thrust of all government interventions has been on imposing their own usually short-term outputs within programmes aimed at communities.

'I think the sense of having community workers that are accountable to local communities is something that has been diluted because of this project-driven culture.' (Gersh Subhra)

For the community or employing agency to continue to receive their funding, they must provide evidence that they have met the outputs to which they have agreed. For community development, providing this evidence has posed real challenges, as suggested by Jerry Smith above. Christine Dixon highlights the need to be looking for relevant evidence in the context of a long-term process:

'I would like more people to realise by doing this kind of work there are good outcomes. There are more outcomes actually in the long run but it can take a lot longer. But it's going to be stronger if you do it this way. When people say, "how many organisations have you developed", I'd say "community development doesn't necessarily lead to a long-term organisation". In some ways if you push too hard for measurements you can get the wrong things. The measurements can be a restriction in themselves.'

Measuring confidence and empowerment is not about counting buttons. It requires a much broader understanding of what counts as evidence. Evaluation frameworks such as that of ABCD (Barr and Hashagen, 2000) and LEAP (Barr and Dailly, 2008), which have begun to appear in recent years, have contributed a great deal to improving practitioners' ability to evaluate their work.

However, the emphasis on outputs has been challenged by many within the community development field as skewing what we do and what we value. Mandy Wilson links the emphasis on outputs to the funding regimes behind community development such as the Single Regeneration Budget (SRB):

> 'Those outputs have no relation with community development and I think SRB particularly has created a culture where people think in terms of outputs. People don't think enough about the difference they're trying to make personally.' (Mandy Wilson)

While we need to record activities and services, the emphasis on this in itself may detract from the end goals, as Mandy suggests. Our efforts should be directed towards making sure that programmes and initiatives contain the right outcomes – the outcomes that reflect the needs and wishes of the communities in which practitioners are working.

> 'I think you can find the outputs and not really be measuring the long-term outcomes. We have to get the outputs right in order to get our money but there's no point having the money if the outcomes are not what we were hoping they would be and you simply can't measure those over a short timeframe.' (David Robinson)

So how is that done? Alan Barr suggests a starting point, although warns us against false hopes of tackling entrenched problems:

> 'It's about saying, "what's the problem we've got here, what's the change that we want to create that will satisfy us that we have dealt with the problem in a way that reflects the aspirations of the people we're working with". I don't think we should delude ourselves that the kinds of things that can cause people difficulty are susceptible to absolute solutions.'

The avenue that is on offer today for communities and practitioners is to participate within the community planning structures provided by government. Currently, efforts are being made to facilitate community involvement in neighbourhood management structures where it is hoped they will be able to contribute towards setting outcomes and priorities that will be passed upwards. It is too soon to tell whether these structures will enable such a degree of influence for communities.

Georgina Webster suggests that practitioners need to challenge outputs and outcomes that do not fit with what community development is about or what communities want. They should suggest realistic alternatives:

> 'I think we have lost a degree of assertion. What community development needs to be saying is, "those outputs that you are asking of us aren't relevant but this one is relevant". Community workers always say, "they expect us to achieve this in a year, but it takes years before you can achieve anything". Absolutely right. However, in a year, you should be able to show something. People get scared because they're given outputs that are totally inappropriate.'

As mentioned in the previous chapters, there may be more opportunity and scope for practitioners to challenge than is currently recognised and to ensure, as Georgina suggests, that the outputs are appropriate and relevant. It is about establishing what and where those parameters are and working to push these outwards. While there are structural difficulties, practitioners need to be both assertive and tactical in their efforts to influence these structures. We need also to acknowledge the community organising and campaigning work that is happening today through non-state-funded groups, many of who are able to adopt such a stance.

Practising community development during the 1980s funded through government, Charlie Jordan describes how he was working strategically to try and find a way through these tensions:

> 'There was a sense that we were using government money subversively in those days by putting down a number of words on a bit of paper that were acceptable. Our long-term objectives were about building a sustainable community activity with the emergence of a group of leaders, building organisational structures that were capable of representing local people's views and getting into strong negotiating positions in order to negotiate better capital spend which would improve the quality of services locally. Those were

our long-term aims but they were never spelt out. What we put down on a bit of paper was to do with setting up local community groups that is what we did. By the time that we were two years in, the longer term strategy was becoming evident and people became uneasy about it.'

Another approach adopted to positively influence the community outcomes within government programmes includes selling the value of community development to policy makers and funders. In this sense, community development tries to speak the language of policy, to demonstrate how it can deliver what government wants. This is an approach adopted by the national organisations for community development in which they also link the benefits of community development with the long-term processes that produce them. For example, *The community development challenge* report, commissioned and published by the Department for Communities and Local Government (CDF et al, 2006) articulates six components of community development, each of which has specific outcomes that resonate with a policy audience. These outcomes range from an increase in volunteering and the building of social capital through to improving public service delivery and promoting more coherent and effective public policy.

Sustainability

Within the community development field there is a consensus on the need for sustained, long-term work:

'I believe very strongly that in-out kind of involvement in people's lives is not very helpful and a lot of those with whom we work have been let down in the past. If you look at some of the young people now, people that are involved in running youth activities, they have been involved with us literally since they were Sure Start age group but there wasn't a Sure Start in those days. I think they would talk about their lives being different from the lives of siblings or others around them. I don't think that would have been the case had their involvement with us been more superficial. It is important as a fixed and stable resource. I think community development has suffered over the years from the idea that this is something you could do for a short period of time.' (David Robinson)

Communities themselves often understand the need for long-term work. It seems only to be policy makers that fail to understand what community development is. Or, is it simply that government funds community development workers to achieve its own objectives and focuses on cost-effective interventions? Much is made of the lack of evidence for community development (in the short term) but community development is a long-term process and I wonder what level of evidence will convince government to fund for the long term. Perhaps in the current economic climate, only evidence relating to community development's impact on employment and economic indicators will be noticed.

Many voluntary and community organisations are able to create opportunities for sustained community development input through juggling funding and going along with the pretence that projects are new when actually they reflect tried and tested work that has been around for a while. Through these convoluted processes emerge the outcomes that resonate with communities. Many community organisations struggle to achieve this balancing act and either continue to live on a shoestring or find themselves delivering government programmes that bring in funding to the organisation.

Let us return to the example of the new neighbourhood structures for devolved decision making to communities. It is to such structures that much community development activity will increasingly be directed as workers try to support the involvement and effective participation of community members. While the language of localism and neighbourhood control rightly meets with approval and optimism we must also analyse these structures to see if they will deliver the changes that communities want. Through such structures, the government hopes that deprived communities will take greater responsibility for their own affairs, managing and running services that were once the domain of public authorities. Community empowerment is not conceived as an end in itself but advanced in the hope that it will promote self-help and enable communities to provide for their own welfare. Is that what communities want and why they wish to get involved? Is that what community development practice ought to be orientated towards? The language of localism is attractive but we should question whether it equates or competes with the aims of social justice and equality.

Competing interests

In Newcastle in the 1980s Ann Chapman recognised the different interests of the community and the local authority and took an approach that involved running two systems of reporting:

> 'This is what we're doing in terms of community work principles and this is how we're selling it to the local authority.'

Working in a climate of cuts, Ann and her colleagues sought to demonstrate their achievements and the value of their work to the different policy agendas and interests while trying to avoid being controlled by them.

Bob Holman suggests that government does not trust people to make the right decisions. He makes a crucial point about the conflict between local priorities and those of national government:

> 'The trouble is that if local residents made decisions, it's not the same targets (as those of government). There is a particular dilemma in neighbourhood work in that neighbourhood bodies, FARE being a good example, don't want to be specific bodies. Say for example, we get a target to reduce drug offending by 25% or we'll reduce the number of kids who go into custody by 50%. We don't want to be that kind of agency because that specialised agency would not gain local support of a holistic nature. You've got to serve the neighbourhood. You must get the backing of the whole neighbourhood. So that is why the agenda of a local committee often clashes with a national agenda and why they don't get grants.'

Similarly, Frances Clarke working in the East End of London acknowledges the different interests of funders and community organisations and how these impact on what type of practice takes place:

> 'Targets make it much harder. If you're trying to meet the outputs of some big programmes they're not likely to correspond exactly with what you want to do. It's probably skewing funding towards service delivery and away from

empowerment type activities where you can't predict what
the outputs will be.'

Funders, agencies and communities all have different agendas. Does
funding and government sponsorship deflect communities and
practitioners away from their agenda for change towards government
priorities for engagement? Have we lost sight of the goals that formed
our original motivation?

Reaching agreement with communities

Expectations have been placed on communities for many years to
contribute to tackling their own problems though working together
with community development professionals. In the 1970s and 1980s,
when workers were producing community newspapers, community
members were involved in producing and delivering the newsletters.
Working with key people in the community was seen as crucial to
establishing trust and providing routes into the community for the
practitioner.

In order to meet these expectations it was felt that communities
needed specific inputs to build their capacity. As a senior community
worker for the Nottingham Community Project in the early 1980s,
Jerry Smith recalls a contracts unit that pioneered agreements between
community workers and community organisations:

> 'Instead of going into an area and saying right, "we're here
> for two years like it or leave it", you would draw up a
> contract with an existing community group and they would
> say what they wanted from you and you would negotiate
> with them as to what you would provide in terms of hours,
> the kind of input they needed, what training they wanted
> and you would write it up as a binding contract, renewable
> after six months if both sides still wanted to.'

While not necessarily in the form of contracts, this more 'professional'
relationship specifying inputs has taken root within the field of capacity
building but less so in generic community development. A much greater
focus on training and skills for community activists combined with a
focus on community asset building are examples of this recent trend.

The concept of new relationships based on expectations was also
evident in the community work approach of Community Links.
Recognising that people's basic needs around housing and welfare

need to be resolved before you can expect them to become involved, Community Links has developed services based on the concept of partnership between the provider and recipient (what some today call 'co-production'):

> 'What we've tried to do in advice work is to say we are equals and that people who are seeking advice do have knowledge that other people don't have. It's a partnership and we've embedded that in the way we work. We've tried to move away from the model of professional and client.' (Frances Clarke)

Adopting this approach, Community Links has successfully involved large numbers of clients to advise and support others in the community.

With a current policy emphasis on the importance of the neighbourhood, government expectations of the role of communities have grown considerably. While the examples above recognise that individuals and communities have skills and knowledge to tackle problems within their communities, we need to be careful that this does not undermine what deprived communities should be able to demand as a right that other more affluent communities take for granted:

> 'If I went in to see my solicitor I wouldn't expect them to say, "what I will do is show you how to be able to do it yourself". What should people have the right to be able to expect to get out of professions? There is a tension between sometimes expecting this in disadvantaged working-class communities where it is not what we would apply for the middle-class community.' (Brian Astin)

The balance between self-help and rights is particularly challenging today. The language of community responsibility and empowerment is seductive but can also blind us to the broader responsibilities, beyond individuals and communities, which lie with the different tiers and facets of government. Community development would always advocate the active participation of communities but we need to be realistic about what is being asked of communities and whether they are able and willing to perform these roles.

Community development process

What has the emphasis on upward accountability meant for community development? Ashok Ohri makes a key point:

> 'There was definitely a need for more accountability of community workers but if accountability has meant that we have lost the opportunity to engage in a process then we have lost community development.'

There has most certainly been a shift away from a more open-ended form of practice to one in which practitioners need to deliver outputs and meet targets. The 'animating' role in which practitioners would pose questions and encourage community members to think and act on issues important to them is disappearing amidst the need to deliver tangible outcomes. Community development is now much more project-driven in which funded projects need to be delivering from day one. This contrasts sharply with earlier generic practice which, while less accountable, did provide practitioners with flexibility in how they worked:

> 'There's a real sense that community work has gone into fast-forward and that practitioners are having to work much more quickly through the stages of community work with the result that you skip stages.' (Gersh Subhra)

This 'speeded up' process of community development in response to the demand for greater upward accountability poses challenges for the fundamentals of community development. Empowering the 'community' to do it their way and take decisions becomes more difficult as outputs and targets need to be set:

> 'You didn't do it for them [community groups]. If they needed to produce a leaflet you sat down with them, no matter how long it took, you would get them to do the leaflet.' (Charlie Garratt)

The practitioner can easily be enticed to step in and do it *for* the community. Bob Holman spent much of his 10 years on the Easterhouse Estate in Glasgow enabling local people to present their own views to national bodies and policy makers of what life was like on the ground rather than interpreting and doing the talking himself. This takes considerable time and effort yet ensures that what is presented is rooted in real-life experiences. Andy Wiggans refers to enabling people to 'make words speak', which is a wonderful way of describing how community development can help people to find the words and enable them to speak.

Looking back, Jerry Smith sees patience as a crucial requirement of a successful practitioner:

> 'The temptation is always, because you can do it quicker and perhaps you've got the contacts that they haven't, to cut corners and do it yourself. This is the thing that's held community development back more than anything over the years. Too many community workers just don't have enough patience.'

This temptation is stronger today with the pressure of targets but it has always been a tricky dilemma. Brian Astin provides us with an example that makes the point well. He recalls a local campaign to stop the closure of a primary school, organised by the project in which he worked, together with the local community. Brian highlights the tensions between wanting to enable local people to develop skills and working against a set timetable:

> 'If we'd have worked to the community development principles, the local community might have developed skills but the school might have been closed down because we might not have been able to act at the right time and at the right meetings. I don't think the local community who were very keen not to see the school closed would have thanked us if we had said that "we've learnt a lot but unfortunately you lost the school.'

Practitioners who worked in the 1970s and 1980s recall having the time to build relationships and how this was a key aspect of their work:

> 'You could just spend half a day with somebody who was upset and talk it through with them, or after somebody stormed out of a meeting the night before, I could go round the next morning and say, should we have a cup of coffee and talk about this? I spent a lot of time just talking to people in their homes really.' (Mandy Wilson)

Charlie Garratt recalls that, in the early 1980s, he and other community workers with whom he worked were assigned to supporting and developing two community organisations each, which allowed the practitioner sufficient time to get to know everyone involved in the group and to work intensively with groups on what they were trying to achieve.

Neighbourhood work

Developing relationships with members of the community was central to the practice of community development in the context of neighbourhood work during the 1970s and 1980s. It was recognised that the work could not be done from a distance and that practitioners had to be in the neighbourhoods, getting to know people and listening to what they had to say. While in some cases practitioners actually lived within the communities in which they worked, this was not the norm and the dominant neighbourhood work approach consisted of making contact with people, for example by knocking on people's doors, and working with them on what they needed:

> 'Some of the beginnings were about rolling your sleeves up and getting started with what was there. I remember a year or two's worth of knocking on doors, chatting to people in the pub, trying to encourage three people to take a lead and then organising a meeting and putting some leaflets round in the working men's clubs and pubs – "do you want to come together and form a bit of an association and try and improve things round here?" It was a very open-ended sort of thing.' (Tony Herrmann)

In Lambeth, Christine Dixon recognised the need to be close to what was happening within communities, rather than once removed in what at the time were called 'neighbourhood councils'. Christine would make her initial contacts by sitting in on advice sessions within the local advice centre and listening to what community members felt while helping out in the centre. It is perhaps more difficult for practitioners today to work in this way as they have less flexibility yet much greater expectations from the funder and employing agency. Has the importance of listening to and understanding what communities are saying and how they define their problems been overlooked in favour of a more technical exploration to developing relationships and involving communities?

To understand what communities are saying, practitioners need to be curious. They need to have a desire to listen and make sense of what people are going through and what motivates them. Neighbourhood practice was based on understanding people's experiences and developing working relationships with them to try to change whatever was causing the problem:

> 'I remember it as trying to understand what the experience was that people were having. It was about trying to get in touch with what was causing them difficulty and think as they would think about that experience, but bringing to bear a degree of knowledge and skills in how you achieve the kind of change that you're looking for.' (Alan Barr)

Understanding communities also develops through working alongside them. Andy Wiggans reflects that for him one of the main parts of the community development job was to do the "unbrilliant things", to put yourself out to help someone. If you were willing and able to 'roll up your sleeves' and do the 'unbrilliant things', it provided the practitioner with the scope with which to carve out a role, as experienced by Tony Herrmann:

> 'People didn't see me as a council officer. They might have seen other people as council officers, but I was pretty much me. They saw me as somebody who could help, somebody who knew things, who could get things sorted, somebody who was useful.'

The idea of the practitioner helping out and being a resource within communities is dependent on their ability to spend time within communities and to have the freedom to respond accordingly, neither of which are in great supply for practitioners today. However, while the quality of these relationships may have weakened, there has certainly been a considerable broadening over the past 30 years in terms of who benefits from community development support:

> 'Community work is now much more inclusive. It is happening with a much broader range of communities than it used to, including the most marginalised such as refugees, and asylum seekers, lesbians and gay men, homeless people, Travellers, people on the margins of society.' (Georgina Webster)

This opening up of community development to ensure that all parts of the community can access and benefit from community development input is perhaps one of the most significant advances in terms of community development practice. Issues of equality and diversity are now at the forefront of today's practice (Gilchrist, 2007).

Capacity building and involvement

Before we describe the role of the practitioner in terms of community involvement, it is important to refer briefly to the role of capacity building in communities. A key element within the neighbourhood approach was the development of community-based organisations. Through bringing people together and identifying common needs, the worker would assist in formalising the group to create an organisation to try and influence on behalf of the community. Today, the capacity building of community organisations is an increasingly dominant aspect of the work of practitioners. Alan Barr expresses a growing concern for many about how capacity building today is being delivered:

> 'People learn in the process of doing things. You build the capacity you need to do the things that you want to do and you shouldn't try and build capacity beyond that which we want to do at the time.'

Thus, issues about constitutions, policies and money are only relevant if they are needed by the community group to achieve the change that they have identified. Capacity building today appears to place an over-emphasis on technical issues and is in danger of losing touch with what communities and community organisations are trying to achieve.

In the past, as with practice today, a great deal of effort was spent trying to involve people in community activities and decision making within their local areas. The methods used in the past were perhaps more responsive to how local people wanted to get involved and were less formal:

> 'Maybe the last thing they've [the community] got the energy or time for is to come to your meeting. Maybe we'll do a different kind of meeting, we'll have a street meeting. We used to build inflatables long before you could buy them and put them in community centres. We knew that you could take one of those, no leaflets, nothing needed, and go and park it somewhere on the estate. We would

ask someone if we can run a lead into your back kitchen, bring some orange juice and some tea, whatever. Within 20 minutes, instant meeting. Kids have a bit of fun as well, everybody happy.' (Andy Wiggans)

Similarly, Mandy Wilson recalls how she got homeless people involved in housing campaigns:

'We went down with a larger hailer and a double-decker bus and parked the double-decker bus outside the DHSS on a Thursday when we knew the homeless people were going to get their giros. We offered them cups of coffee and all that kind of stuff. They all came on the bus and we chatted to them and on the day of the meeting I got lots of advice workers to come and we went round Stratford Broadway and all along the Romford Road with a loudhailer shouting the meeting is now, come on. We got loads of people. They wouldn't have come if I hadn't gone to pick them up.'

Key to these experiences of involving people was the sheer determination and creativity on the part of the practitioner to get individuals and communities involved and the time spent building relationships and getting to know people well. Importantly, the approaches were based on an understanding of the stage of development people had reached – and responded accordingly – rather than starting at the point of involvement. David Robinson recounts how his practice has encouraged involvement:

'You don't start off by saying "get involved in the Local strategic partnership". The local authority has nothing to offer some of those with whom we are working. You start off by addressing their immediate needs that are filling their every waking moment and over time you are able to demonstrate that you can make things work together and we can achieve some change. People begin to appreciate their own power and confidence builds with that and as a final product involvement flows from that. It's not something that a community development worker needs to do, it follows from doing all the rest really well.'

There is, however, plenty of scope within the existing structures to ensure that communities are not dictated to and are able to voice their wants and needs. This opportunity requires, as in the past, a level of determination, creativity and political nous on the part of the practitioner:

> 'At the beginning of the LSP [local strategic partnership] we had 12 neighbourhood facilitators supporting 12 area forums. One neighbourhood worker was a really gifted community worker and went out and involved everyone in the forum. We used to get 250 people coming to meetings telling officers what the issues were. It was exactly the same as the Tower Blocks campaign: this is the issue on our doorstep, this is what we want to be done and the officers were really called to account. If you didn't have a good community worker you would have probably said it's just people sat round a table making decisions for everyone else.' (Frances Clarke)

For community involvement to have a benefit for communities themselves they need the support from 'gifted' community workers as described above, individuals who can encourage communities to express their concerns in their own words. This support must be twinned with a recognition that communities get involved in order to see changes happen in their area, not to comment on how well, or not, an authority has performed:

> 'The scope for people to get involved has grown but the support infrastructure to help them do that is not necessarily there or where it has grown it's been short term. The consultation activity around individual initiatives are greater than they used to be and certainly much more sophisticated in terms of approaches, but in some ways much more short term. It's about consultation, rather than long-term involvement and engagement.' (Brian Astin)

Perhaps it is important to ask ourselves to what extent the characteristics of a good community worker described here (patience, determination, creativity) give a value and prominence in community development training and programmes? These characteristics would certainly resonate with the wishes of the communities in which practitioners are based, but perhaps sit less easily with the needs of government programmes?

Practice today places an emphasis on how to train and develop the skills of active community members, often referred to as activists, to participate effectively within the structures provided. An increasing emphasis is being placed on the role of the community activists who are being used as representatives, trainers and consultants within their own communities. Activists appear to be playing a stronger role within community development today and adopting roles similar to those of the paid community development workers.

For some, the increasing importance of activists suggests a change in role for the paid practitioners. Others suggest that the role always has been, and always will be, very different:

> 'There is always a risk with community activists that they become very single-minded and focused on the thing they want to achieve. It takes a lot of energy, commitment and objectivity to be able to open yourself up to the other issues. The difference is becoming part of the shin-kicking crowd or being able to develop an open and objective relationship even with the organisations with whom you may have a problem. I think community development workers are naturally expected to be able to do that, it's part of their role.' (Judy Yacoub)

Community activists are a valuable resource for the community development worker but it is important that they do not become a cost-effective solution for work within communities while community development workers disappear into policy and planning roles. Community development workers need to be rooted in communities yet working strategically to enable communities to achieve the changes they articulate. This will require an accountability to the community equivalent to that of accountability to the sponsor and a willingness for practitioners to challenge and negotiate for communities rather than simply preparing communities for policy implementation.

SEVEN

Where is community development today?

Colleagues have suggested to me that community development has arrived at the policy table. Interviews with experienced practitioners and observation of current practice suggests that it is the importance of 'community' to the New Labour government that has arrived and not that of community development. It is the newer categories of 'community engagement' and 'community empowerment' that underpin the 2006 local government White Paper (CLG, 2006) and not that of community development.

So what is community engagement about and how does it link to community development? The terminology of engagement and involvement emerged most recently in the context of a crisis of legitimacy facing the state, particularly within disadvantaged communities. Voting turnout has been at an all time low, while public services have been rocked by the challenges of cuts and reform. Engagement of the public in the democratic process and also in easing the burden on public services underpins the rhetoric. Community engagement connects with an emphasis on a new social contract between the individual and the state in which individuals are expected to contribute something in return for quality services – 'a something for something society'.

Community engagement and participation are therefore about communities and individuals helping themselves. Rather than enabling communities to have control over resources and institutions, engagement is framed in terms of promoting personal responsibility and behaviour change on the part of deprived communities. This resonates with an underpinning ideology of social pathology that has existed throughout the period covered by our interviews and challenged only by the structural analysis of the national community development project (CDP). The essence of this ideology is that poor people are to blame for their own circumstances and thus need to take greater responsibility.

While the link between community development and community engagement has not been made explicit, one can see quite clearly that support for community projects, which promote participation and self-help twinned with capacity building of the voluntary and community sector to deliver services, fits squarely with the policy interests behind engagement. In fact, much of community development practice today works towards these goals. What was previously coined the 'state community strategy' by Paul Corrigan has been given new vigour, with the voluntary and community sector playing a much higher profile in delivering services on contract to local authorities and partnership agencies.

The context of community engagement provides community development with opportunities to promote community-based activity and solutions to local issues. Engagement and participation do not just happen effortlessly but are the products of sustained and effective community development. The challenge is to ensure that the community solutions that are developed are in response to issues that communities themselves judge to be important. Can community development do more to exploit the space that engagement provides, narrow though it may be, to promote community needs and wants rather than policy requirements, and to enable communities to achieve greater control and ownership over decision-making structures?

Despite this clear connection, community development still appears to be knocking on the door rather than sitting at the table. Why is this, given the pivotal role it seems to occupy? It has been suggested that community development lacks an evidence base for its activity, while there are also concerns that it may be too slow a process to achieve the outputs that government demands within the timescales that the political process requires. Perhaps community development lacks recognition simply because it is not understood to be significantly different from either involvement or engagement agendas? The incorporation of community development may have hidden what is actually distinctive about it as a process for facilitating social change on behalf of communities. Less and less do we ask 'why community development?', avoiding any potential tensions and creating an illusion that state and community interests are one and the same, thus 'Together We Can'.

Community development may better leverage the role it could play by distinguishing itself from community engagement and participation. The case can and should be made for how community development can deepen democracy and result in more effective community engagement, alongside other benefits. This requires the approach to start from where the community is at and to recognise and work with the tensions between what communities and policy makers want. Government ambitions for widening democracy will fall short if practitioners are confined to implementing change from above and herding communities into structures and forums they neither own nor relate to.

Community development was certainly recognised some years ago as a valuable tool for managing communities and became increasingly integral to government interventions from the Single Regeneration Programme through to the more recent New Deal for Communities. As a result, community development, as with much of the voluntary sector, has become increasingly dependent on government funding and contracts over the past 10 years, which has impacted hugely on the freedom and independence of practitioners and projects alike. With government funding have also come prescriptive targets and outputs, reflecting more the needs of government than those of the community. Thus, the practice of community development faces increasing challenges, none of them new but perhaps more extreme, as to how it marries up the needs of communities with those of its main sponsor.

Despite or because of the increasing incorporation of community development into government agendas, the community development field appears to have lost its way, with little direction or overarching purpose. Based on a process of social change for the benefit of communities, community development has moved away from what were felt by many to be 'idealistic' goals in the 1970s of reducing poverty and inequalities. These have been replaced by a more 'realistic' focus on involvement within participation structures to influence the quality and delivery of public services. Undoubtedly, there have been significant wins in terms of improvements in public service attitudes but a context of growing wealth inequality, declining social mobility and persistent poverty for millions of people remains unaltered. To what extent should the community development field be raising these issues and developing practice which enables communities to come together to voice their concerns?

This further incorporation and more 'pragmatic' style of community development today is characteristic of wider societal change in which debate, pressure and conflict have dissipated. We can see, however, the re-emergence of such pressure in the form of the considerable anti-war campaigns alongside growing movements to challenge health and education reforms. Community development in the 1970s was a lot about campaigning and lobbying local government for resources for communities in which pressure was viewed as a key ingredient to deliver change. Community development had links with social movements and the unions to whom it turned for support and inspiration. This more radical focus to community development changed enormously with the move towards partnerships and the shift of public resources towards the private sector over these years. Today, it could be argued that national community development agencies focus their energies on realigning community development with evolving government priorities in the hope it may be seated at the table and receive the recognition and security, craved for so long.

The loss of direction and desire to fit in on the part of community development has made it more difficult for practitioners to question and challenge on behalf of communities. This is not to say that it never happens, but the overriding culture is one of compliance and implementation. Perhaps practitioners themselves can be more assertive and ensure they are not self-censoring but this cannot be done alone and requires clearer statements in policy and practice material, outlining what community development stands for rather than what it falls for. This requirement is difficult in a context in which community development is so dependent on government funding.

The community development profession seems to work on what government pays for and fails to plan in any strategic manner for what it wants to achieve. As a result, the community development field displays insecurity, a lack of confidence and confusion. Current concerns focus on how community development can demonstrate its 'value-added' to government targets rather than to the community. The responsibility for this lack of independence lies with the community development field, not simply with government.

The focus on government priorities has had major implications for the day-to-day practice of community development. We are witnessing the disappearance of community development as a 'process' as described in earlier chapters and the 'speeding up' of community development into a short-term intervention. Practitioners have less time to develop relationships within communities to do what Andy Wiggans describes as the 'unbrilliant things', as focus is switched to ensuring successful delivery of project outputs. The development of relationships within communities is fundamental to good community development and is about enabling communities to articulate what they want to change and to support them (often through community-based organisations or campaigns) to achieve these changes. The process can become an educational and empowering one for those involved. Ironically, this shift in practice is likely to limit the impact that community development can have on government ambitions to strengthen democracy and community development may find itself in the unenviable position of having to constantly adapt to prove its worth to government, while moving away from the very approach which may bring success.

In place of spending time with communities, practitioners spend more time at their desks and in meetings. The role of the practitioner has become more managerial, with workers focusing on capacity building, funding, policy development and implementation. For example, the focus on the theme of involvement requires practitioners to spend more time managing the relationships between communities and authority and managing the information flows from one to another. This role has been accurately described by one interviewee as a 'liaison officer' for government.

The previously accepted norm that a community development worker needed to be based in the community long term has been undermined by the shift to a contract-based culture. Practitioners are unable to engage in an organic process within communities. Instead, issues need to be defined and packaged into time, outputs and indicators beforehand. Relationships and community capacity develop over years, not overnight. Crucially, narrowing the practice of community development in this way makes it much more difficult for practitioners to act as social change agents within communities and places them in a removed role in which they struggle to fit community needs and wishes into policy objectives.

The loss of focus on social change is reflected in a more technicalised approach to community development training in which emphasis is placed on the techniques and toolkits for engagement rather than how you mobilise communities around common concerns and enable them to plan strategically. Practice development and practice theory are not investment priorities for employing agencies whose focus is on securing funding and contracts through the delivery of outputs.

These changes in terms of purpose, practice, training and funding have begun to strip community development of its political analysis. Tony Herrmann recalls that in the 1970s it was clear what it meant to be a community worker whereas today he feels compelled to ask more questions of the worker he meets. While there are most certainly individual practitioners out there who still work with a political understanding to their role, it is also the case that many do not and are encouraged to view their role as one of delivery and implementation. It is hard to envisage how practitioners and the community development profession will build the confidence and sense of purpose to achieve changes with communities without also reconnecting with the politics of community development.

Where is community development headed?

The policy context for community development in the near future is likely to remain that of promoting community engagement within public services. The 2006 local government White Paper (CLG, 2006) introduced a statutory duty to 'inform, consult, involve and devolve' to communities, making particular reference to 'hard-to-reach' communities. Emphasis is placed within the document on pursuing the devolution agenda and the language of 'community empowerment' and some statutory services such as youth facilities may be handed down for communities to take over the running.

While driven by a government aim to reform and make savings in public services, perhaps this context also provides community development with an opportunity to bring real meaning and purpose to the language of involvement. To meaningfully engage what are referred to as 'hard-to-reach' communities will require policy and practice which addresses the day-to-day reality facing deprived communities. Community development practitioners may choose to focus on enabling disadvantaged and marginalised communities to have real voice and influence. This will require a more challenging style of practice which rejects the incorporation of communities into the agenda of the state and promotes the interests and concerns of communities.

There is little evidence to date of community involvement resulting in community influence over decisions. Few communities have any real power as control from the centre remains strong. Tokenism is often mentioned in the context of community involvement, to which the cure is seen to be capacity building of the community to help them better understand the system. Genuine community development approaches aimed at facilitating positive change with communities have the potential to breathe life into these initiatives but will undoubtedly require challenge and change for all involved. Authorities and partnerships will need to be able to listen and act on views and voices that dissent from the policy agenda rather than silence such opinions.

There must be devolution of power not just responsibility. In Luton, the Marsh Farm Community Trust has received considerable attention for its efforts to organise the local community to become active and responsible, taking decisions and influencing the planning and delivery of services in the area. The success of the Trust is based on considerable effort to mobilise the community and to work tirelessly to devolve both power and resources to the community. This example has been based on many hours of community work and is about developing new mechanisms for community democracy which change how communities relate to the local state. It is not an easy answer but one in which struggles over power and influence are central and acknowledged.

Community ownership and control may be the opportunity but there also exists an increasing threat posed by what is referred to as the 'diversity and choice' agenda. Local authorities are being redefined into commissioning agents and moving away from being the main provider of public services in an area. While some services, as mentioned above, are being contracted to the voluntary sector, there is also an increasing role for the private sector in the ownership and delivery of public services. Core elements of what are regarded as the local state such as schools and hospitals are being privatised in the quest for reform and savings. The increasing role of the private sector poses a serious contradiction for the themes of community involvement and engagement as ownership for services lies outside of the local state. What scope will communities have to influence and make such services accountable to local needs and wants? Local democratic control is likely to dwindle as more and more services are delivered through the market. How will community development be practised in such a context, and is the model of community planning still the most relevant in such circumstances?

The focus on engagement will be accompanied by a shift in practice away from working within communities, so that community development is increasingly concerned with assisting the various institutions which touch the lives of communities to better engage. Thus, community development may well become more evident within services such as health, education, police and planning. There is a great deal of value in assisting such institutions to better involve and listen to community views, but we must not confuse such engagement practice with the process of social change that defines community development.

The current emphasis on spreading community development techniques to other professions raises interesting issues about what it is that is being shared. Many organisations may neither sign up to nor apply the values of community development, so what is it they are left practising? Without these values is it still community development? Perhaps in the quest to advance community development as an appropriate approach for other sectors, we need also to establish the starting conditions for an effective community development process. Can it simply be applied anywhere, anyhow and explained away as adapting to circumstance? We may also benefit from clarifying what is not negotiable when exporting community development to other professions.

The focus of community development practice on institutions will coincide with a push for practitioners to work on area-based policy and strategy addressing implementation gaps. What will this mean for practice? In this context, we can assume that practitioners will have even less of a presence at community level and their work will be defined ever more by policy requirements than community needs. Working on the implementation of 'community' policies across areas fits with a familiar approach in which the problems faced by communities are defined from above in the form of outputs and targets. Community development will continue to strive for better evidence of its impact and expend much energy in how it can demonstrate it is meeting government targets. Communities will be encouraged to influence the targets set at a local level. In this context, it is hard to see how community development practitioners will forge closer working alliances with the communities in which they practice, and what voice communities will actually have.

Assuming practitioners move towards a 'coordinating' role, who will be working at the grass roots? The government has put much emphasis on involving and employing resident activists and there is a likelihood that community members/volunteers will be called on to carry out a neighbourhood work role that was previously the task of community development workers. This chimes with policy reference to community development as a 'resource-neutral' activity.

The greater prominence of community activists is accompanied by a revived role for local councillors within the 2006 White Paper (CLG, 2006). Councillors are positioned as the democratic champion and voice of communities with control of a small budget and able to instigate a 'councillor call for action' to take forward community concerns and suggestions to local authorities and other providers. Thus, councillors may become important allies for communities and practitioners and the relationships at this level will be essential to influence upwards. This significant role for councillors alongside activists represents a shift from the earlier history of community development. Practitioners, activists and local communities would be wise to plan together how they can make the most of this revived role for local councillors to achieve the changes they seek.

The future for community development looks bleak, with practitioners facing increasing challenges in how they work according to the values and methods of community development. The threat of an even further reduced community presence for practitioners looms large. Practitioners and their representative organisations, together with communities, need to exploit the opportunities and tensions thrown up by the emerging new context. The government is still struggling to make engagement a reality for many communities and there is little sign of an upturn in civic participation or trust in political institutions. Community development can forge alliances with communities, community organisations and campaigns, activists, councillors, unions and other local institutions to make the rhetoric of engagement and involvement mean something real to local communities.

The community development field must stand up and challenge on the basis of community concerns, which may mean assisting local campaigns rather than ducking difficult issues. Community development is by its very nature a political practice which requires practitioners and agencies to work with communities to help them to plan for and win greater power and influence over their lives. The process is empowering for those that get involved as they challenge their own and societal views of them as victims, realising that many others face the same difficulties and thus begin to demand change. Emptying community development to become little more than a vessel for engagement in government agendas misses the huge potential that community development offers and will result in its slow death as a process for real change within and for communities.

Lessons to guide the practice of community development

So what can we learn from the experiences and insights of those practitioners working in the 1970s and 1980s? What can their experiences show us for how we can strengthen the position and role of community development for the coming years? Six lessons emerge which, while not comprehensive, hopefully provide us with a useful guide.

1. Clarify the 'why' of community development

The community development field needs to rediscover what the community development approach is for, and decide what the role of the community development practitioner is. Just as we experience today, tensions existed in the past between what the state wanted from community development and community aspirations of community development. Tensions have existed for many years between those who see community development as a tool to help communities better cope with the reality they face and those who view community development as a method to enable communities to challenge and change this reality. The latter position has been weakened with the realisation that community development alone is not the route to eradicating structural poverty and deprivation and that this is dependent on complex relationships between local, national and international actors and strategies.

Perhaps the thought that community development could radically alter local problems of which the root causes lay elsewhere was naïve given the limited resources that have always been invested in community development. This is not to say that we should give up pursuing goals of social justice and equality and that community development has nothing to offer such a cause. For community development to make even a minor inroad into the entrenched poverty and deprivation faced by many communities it requires a clear and unwavering purpose backed up by strategies and actions that justify hope. No, it cannot be done alone, but together with other civil society organisations, unions and political actors it stands a chance to make a difference of which it can be proud.

To arrive at such a consensus within the community development field will be difficult in itself. The bulk of practice today is driven by an end goal of involvement, and there is a disconnection with any aspirations of change. In fact, the present funding climate has resulted in what is referred to as 'mission drift' for many voluntary and community organisations away from their original aims of empowerment and social change towards an ever growing focus on service delivery. Community development itself has become ever more professionalised and appears to attract individuals who are more likely to be looking for a career than having an impact on the housing or social context for a particular community.

However, it is also the case that many practitioners and organisations struggle with a growing split between what they understand to be the aims, values and approach of community development and their day-to-day practice. There is an increased emphasis within practice on implementation of top-down policy priorities and a lack of freedom for workers to support communities to voice their own needs and wants and to act on the issues that they judge to be important. One approach has been for practitioners to 'capacity build' communities to better engage, based on the assumption that the problem lies with the community and their lack of understanding. Not surprisingly, there is little evidence to suggest that this focus on understanding the bureaucracy has brought about the changes that communities wish to see. Changes that deprived communities call for invariably involve money and power which are not often handed over freely on polite request.

Community development is suffering from a crisis of purpose which will not be resolved through further direction from policy makers and government funding. Instead, those working in the field need to take the lead in reconnecting the aims, values and practice of community development. If community development wants to evidence practice it would do well to start by demonstrating how the values and aims of community development can be practised today. From such a review we need to be clear what community development is and what it is not. Perhaps such an openness of debate will result in the emergence of the different views within the community development field and the challenge will be to see whether agreement can be reached regarding what is and is not negotiable in the use and practice of community development and for whom it serves. Avoidance of such an open examination will merely result in community development becoming indistinguishable from government techniques of engagement and involvement and a greater distancing from the communities for whom it can benefit.

2. Plan for change

If the community development field can re-establish its purpose, as suggested above, then it falls to the national organisations representing community development to kick-start attempts at identifying and agreeing ambitious goals for the field for the coming years. It is important that such a process involves views and ideas from smaller and more radical organisations and not just the views of the larger government-funded, community development providers. Community development practitioners and the communities with which they work need to inform this process.

Some of these goals may challenge current government thinking and policy and will therefore require carefully planned strategies in the short, medium and long term. These strategies will, by definition, detail the approaches, resources and capacity needs, training, partners and allies with whom community development must work to realise success. A national strategy will inevitably be removed from the specifics of every locality but such a strategy should be relevant and tailored to local circumstances as well as being informed and influenced by what is happening locally.

Relationships with other organisations and the state at local, regional and national levels will be key. Such planning requires us to think what it is we want from sponsors to help community development achieve its purpose rather than vice versa. It is vital that the community development field builds alliances and forms of organisation that enable communities to define the issues and problems they face for themselves and reverses the current top–down definition of community problems. A difficult issue to face will be that of resourcing for community development. Through such strategies, the community development field needs to negotiate for local and national government funding, not to be led by it. Statutory funding needs to be part of a mix which includes European funds, charitable funding and earned income.

Planning community development at these different levels to achieve both national and local goals based on community needs will encourage the careful deployment of practitioners in organisations where community development can be practised effectively. Basic conditions for effective community development practice should help to reduce many of the current pressures that practitioners experience. Practitioners need to be provided with opportunities to meet with one another in order to discuss approaches and tactics to achieving change, a very different proposition to the coordination of practitioners to facilitate policy implementation.

Through these strategies, it is hoped that community development will have a clear focus and direction while also providing practitioners with a renewed purpose that many are looking for. Accountability to communities rather than just the state will define the strategies and ensure community development has an increased legitimacy and connection within the communities it serves to support.

3. Act politically

Community development is a political process. Much of today's practice (and training) has lost touch with the political nature of community development and treats it as a technical activity for which values and processes are of little importance. Capacity building, for example, makes little reference to the problems that communities face, instead focusing on the bureaucratic remedies of policies and procedures. For some, this is a deliberate attempt to stifle any form of dissent within communities.

Community development is not a neutral activity. It aims to bring about a process of social change through which the positive values of empowerment, equality and self-determination are realised. In the past, links with social and political movements made this aspect of community development more overt. Practitioners tended to hold strong views about social change in which they worked to give voice and power to deprived and marginalised communities.

The context for community development today is different to that of, say, the early 1970s having become more of a career than a movement, yet the political nature is surely still inherent to the process if we are serious about affecting change. The role of the community development practitioner is ultimately about assisting communities to organise themselves in order to positively influence and change their communities rather than be placed in the roles of passive victims of social policy. This process of organisation and empowerment is about accountability, influence, justice and power, all of which are highly political.

The context in which community development operates remains overtly political; we just choose to ignore it. Current social policy which dominates community development practice carries a strong political message. Deprived communities are expected to take greater responsibility as the state withdraws, often hidden within the language of self-help and active citizenship. Current practice can be linked to references about encouraging behaviour change and adaptation on the part of poorer communities. Little mention is made about what such communities should be able to expect from the state. It is important for community development practitioners and theorists to expose these trends and to practise in ways which challenge the pathology underpinning such thinking.

The political nature of community development practice could be seen in the 1970s and 1980s in the form of campaigns and pressure groups. The shift towards the partnership model of working put an end to most, not all, of community campaigning and community action. Bottom-up pressure from communities was replaced by a new form of top-down pressure on not just agencies and practitioners, but also communities who themselves have become an extended arm of the state.

Pressure upwards has been drowned out as communities are encouraged at every opportunity to participate within the systems the state has provided. It is hard to know whether participation is bringing about the power and influence that communities demand, but indications suggest that the engagement experiment may head the same way as previous failed attempts at participation since the 1960s. For some, it is important that practitioners and communities provide evidence to government as to the problems and solutions facing communities, thus the current enthusiasm for what is described as 'evidence-based policy making'. I find the similarity between the experience of CDP in the mid-1970s of raising issues about poverty with policy makers to no avail remarkably similar to the more recent experience of the Joseph Rowntree Foundation-sponsored Power Inquiry into the need for democratic change:

> At the Power Inquiry, we have spent two years listening to people across Britain, recording their evidence and views. We have written a major report, *Power to the people*, which made many suggestions and received warm praise from across Westminster. But nothing has come of it.
>
> We know now that kindly asking political leaders to deliver lasting democratic change does not work. Even when politicians want to help, the British system has an amazing capacity to ruin the outcome. (email from Helena Kennedy QC, Chair, Power Inquiry and Pam Giddy, Director, Power Inquiry, 22 January 2007)

This and other experiences within communities, suggest that community pressure is still just as relevant and for us not to believe the rhetoric that changing times make it no longer relevant. Perhaps the language of 'enemies' used by followers of the writings of Saul Alinsky is somewhat outdated, but there is certainly much to be learnt from experiences of mobilising allies, councillors, officers and others we think will help us achieve the social change goals we have set ourselves.

Community development has much to learn from the tactics of community organising and its emphasis on negotiation from positions of strength rather than grateful participation. Strength for a community or even a profession such as that of community development comes from understanding the power you hold and being clear how to negotiate based on a range of bargaining positions. This is what should be meant when we talk of strategic community development.

Today, we require a political system and culture that accepts that pressure and conflict are healthy signs of an active and vibrant democracy. We also require a healthy scepticism to what is achievable through state planning structures and recognition that incorporation is often the result of such participation. Alan Barr is right to point out what he sees as a key threat:

'The biggest threat is that we will delude ourselves that participatory policies are effective when they're not because we weren't actually asking the question whether they're effective. We will satisfy ourselves with measuring the outputs, not the outcomes and so how many partnerships we've got, how many people are sitting around the table, how many issues have been talked about, not what changed as a result of those processes being in place.'

We must not avoid the political nature of community development and instead start to practice on the basis of understanding how to exert influence and power for best effect.

4. Train practitioners to understand and facilitate social change

Training for community development is in need of a major review to ensure it is providing practitioners with the knowledge and skills they require to work effectively to achieve the positive changes that communities articulate. Interviewees recognised that training has never been great but has shifted over recent years to an over-emphasis on 'how to' techniques and frameworks for evaluation. This focus on a technicalised approach to training supports a more managerialist approach to community development emphasising policy priorities (see also Banks et al, 2003).

Practitioners today are working in a more constrained environment, struggling to reconcile top-down and bottom-up pressures. Training needs to support practitioners to make sense of these tensions and develop ways of working effectively within such contradictions. Through training and support, practitioners need to identify what power and influence they have to further the interests of the communities they support and what space they have to enable communities to voice their concerns and needs.

It is right that practitioners need to learn about the policy context in which they work, both locally and nationally. This is not simply about knowing what they need to implement but understanding how government interprets the 'problem', what government wants from communities, to identify overlaps with community wants but also discrepancies and contradictions that can be exploited for the benefit of communities. This requires a more sophisticated level of training which addresses issues of power analysis and dynamics, policy analysis, negotiation and theories of change.

Community development training must also meet the needs of the newer community activists who have a greater prominence within the community development field. Such training needs to build on their lived experiences through providing opportunities to develop a wider understanding and experience base. While such training may require a greater degree of flexibility it must still develop the skills for facilitating change outlined above and not simply provide a set of technical competencies which opens the door to the assumption that anyone can do community development.

5. Practice for change

Community development operating within the era of partnerships and community planning has been successful in achieving significant improvements in some of our public services. It has done little to impact on a context of increasing inequalities of wealth, health and declining social mobility. The partnership model has its limitations and in some cases restricts communities from arguing for a better quality of life.

Community development needs to plan carefully for how practitioners, together with communities, can work within the context of partnerships to effect change. Negotiation and challenge need to reappear as tactics within the make-up of a community development practitioner. Partnerships are government structures to facilitate the implementation of policy at local levels. Communities and practitioners need to recognise that partnerships do not necessarily hold their interests at heart and that they need to exploit them rather than be controlled by their agenda and priorities.

Practitioners are struggling to allow communities to express themselves and are confined to managing the participation of communities into such structures and keeping a lid on pressures and tensions. Practitioners could work with communities to exert such pressure on partnerships and decision-making bodies as part of a process of negotiation in which it is acknowledged that the state needs the active involvement of communities on a much greater scale. Such a position of strength also comes from practitioners encouraging communities and community organisations to come together, recognising common issues and assisting one another to achieve common goals. This is much more than influencing just the outcomes of the partnership and is more about taking greater control and power of the processes and outcomes of decision making impacting on local communities.

The new commitment to local decision making presents communities and community development with opportunities to influence local priorities and decision making. To realise these opportunities we should not hesitate to defend what we stand for. Community development must be about enabling communities to realise change, not facilitating involvement as an end in itself. It is about enabling communities to state what they want and to defend this approach rather than perpetually worrying about what government wants. It is about encouraging the state to listen to how communities wish to engage – an active state – rather than always expecting 'active citizens' to have to engage with what the state wants them to do. We must be supportive of community empowerment but also realistic of what communities are being expected to do. To do all this, community development can only work through a sustained, ongoing presence which is built on close relationships at the community level – not short-term interventions based on the needs of government programmes.

The biggest challenge to such a way of working lies in the lack of freedom that practitioners are afforded. A much greater accountability in community development, which some see as a necessary development, has meant that practitioners are less able to work organically on the issues that arise from within communities. Generic practice has disappeared from many localities and been replaced by a thematic focus on the likes of crime and community safety or community engagement.

National organisations representing community development need to argue for a greater degree of flexibility and room for practice. Training for community development must support workers to identify ways in which they can create more room for manoeuvre, whether through exploiting the contradictions, improving skills for negotiation or simply hiding some practice behind the veneer of the funded engagement activities. Either way, practitioners themselves will need to take more risks, identify the parameters in which they can operate and try where possible to push these outwards. As Gary Craig asserted in Chapter Four, government is unlikely to offer such freedom so practitioners need to work for it.

Accountability needs to be redirected towards the communities that practitioners serve and not solely upwards to the policies and sponsors that demand compliance. While practitioners can begin to take more challenges, employing organisations, local authorities and national community development organisations need to be making the case for long-term community development instead of short-term, project-based interventions which benefit few. Ashok Ohri's comment (see Chapter Six) that the loss of a process means we have lost community development is an arresting statement that should urge all of us to be fighting for longer-term community development.

The environment for community development practice should also allow time for the development of meaningful relationships within communities. It is widely acknowledged that practitioners today do not have time to listen and understand where communities are at, how they define their difficulties and what solutions they propose. The 'making sense' role that Gary Craig referred to earlier, in which communities begin to understand what is happening within their neighbourhood and why, has been replaced by a narrow focus on delivery and implementation. This educational role to community development is a key feature underpinning any aspirations that government may hold for community empowerment.

The starting point for community development should be where the community is at. David Robinson makes the point clearly in Chapter Six that we need to understand how and when people want to engage, which is likely to be when they have had the problems that concern them day and night met first. Community development that starts at the point of involvement is likely to result in frustration on the part of practitioners and communities. Understanding communities requires that practitioners get closer to communities, not further away, as is the current trend. Support in the form of community capacity building needs to be based on what communities need at a given point to achieve their aims, not delivered to communities as a good in and of itself. Community development needs to get back in touch with the reality and wishes of local communities and for practice to receive its strength from this legitimacy.

In an article in 1997, Mae Shaw put forward a practice framework to address the loss of direction for community work, the basis of which reinforces our learning from practice. What she describes as the 'seven Cs of radical practice' are summarised as: criticality, consciousness, commitment, collectivity, competence, creativity and choice (Shaw, 1997). This framework is a helpful start to discuss and renegotiate the role of practitioners in working for change within communities.

6. Let's start talking

Community development should not be based on idealistic promises with little hope of realisation. It should be based on the goals of social change that communities are able to articulate together with practitioners. It can start this process through debate and discussion within communities, agencies and the community development field as a whole.

My impressions and that of many of the interviewees is that one of the most noticeable changes within practice over the years covered by interviewees has been the disappearance of a vibrant debate over aims, values and approaches. Silence and frustration seem to be the norm in many settings. The lack of debate ensures that community development remains stuck in its present predicament and will fail to fulfil its potential for communities. A debate on community development needs opening which addresses the points raised in this publication and many more questions that practitioners and communities have regarding the role and practice of community development. *The community development challenge* reports have begun to open up some of these conversations which need broadening out to practitioners and policy makers (see CDF et al, 2006; Bowles, 2008; Miller, 2008; Longstaff, 2008a, 2008b).

Such a debate needs to be informed by a recognition that opportunities exist for community development today, other than one-way policy implementation. The involvement agenda for example, presents us with an interesting tension between participation as a way of communities helping themselves or participation as way of strengthening communities' control over state resources and institutions. Similar tensions exist within most policy initiatives and the inevitable dynamic between top-down and bottom-up. It is in these spaces that community development may be able to support communities to push for power and influence rather than receiving delegated responsibilities.

Conclusion

To conclude, the community development field will continue to face severe challenges over the coming years, but at the same time opportunities will present to enable communities to achieve meaningful change. The practice of community development needs re-energising around its core purpose for social change and should begin to reconnect with politics and people rather than responding just to policy. Community development organisations and practitioners have the potential to realise a win–win scenario for both communities and government, but this will require a greater understanding and analysis of the context in which it operates and a willingness to face challenges and take risks in order to improve the reality for many communities.

References

Alexander Report (1975) *Adult education. The challenge of change*, Edinburgh: HMSO.

Alinsky, S.D. (1971) *Rules for radicals: A pragmatic primer for realistic radicals*, New York: Random House.

Archbishop's Commission on Urban Priority Areas (1985) *Faith in the city*, London: Church House Publishing.

Association of Metropolitan Authorities (1989) *Community development: The local authority role*, Luton: LGMB Publications.

Association of Metropolitan Authorities (1993) *Local authorities and community development: A strategic opportunity for the 1990s*, Luton: LGMB Publications.

Banks, S., Butcher, H.L., Henderson, P. and Robertson, J. (eds) (2003) *Managing community practice: Principles, policies and programmes*, Bristol: The Policy Press.

Barclay Report (1982) *Social workers: Their role and tasks*, London: Bedford Square Press.

Barr, A. (1996) *Practising community development*, London: CDF.

Barr, A. and Dailly, J. (2007) *LEAP step-by-step: An introductory guide to the LEAP framework* (2nd edn), London: CDF.

Barr, A. and Dailly, J. (2008) *LEAP: A manual for learning, evaluation and planning in community development*, London: CDF Publications.

Barr, A. and Hashagen, S. (2000) *Achieving better community development: A framework for evaluating community development*, London: CDF Publications.

Bowles, M. (2008) *Community development challenge: Democracy. The contribution of community development to local governance and democracy*, London: CDF.

Bryant, R. (1972) 'Community action', *British Journal of Social Work*, vol 2, no 2, pp 205-15.

Butcher, H., Banks, S., Henderson, P. with Robertson, J. (2007) *Critical community practice*, Bristol: The Policy Press.

Calouste Gulbenkian Foundation (1968) *Community work and social change*, Gulbenkian Report, London: Longman.

Calouste Gulbenkian Foundation (1973) *Current issues in community work*, London: Routledge and Kegan Paul.

Carnegie UK Trust (2007) *A charter for rural communities*, Dunfermline: Carnegie UK Trust.

CDF (Community Development Foundation), CDX (Community Development Exchange), FCDL (Federation for Community Development Learning) and Community Development Challenge Working Group (2006) *The community development challenge*, London: Department for Communities and Local Government.

CDP Inter-project Editorial Team (1977) *Gilding the ghetto: The state and the poverty experiments*, London: Home Office.

CDX (Community Development Exchange) (2001) *Strategic framework for community development*, Sheffield: CDX.

CDX (2006) *What is community development?*, CDX Information Sheet.

Chanan, G. (1992) *Out of the shadows*, Dublin: Foundation for the Improvement of Living and Working Conditions.

CLG (Communities and Local Government) (2006) *Strong and prosperous communities*, Local Government White Paper, London: CLG.

CLG (2008) *The government's response to the Commission on Integration and Cohesion*, 4 February, London: CLG.

Craig, G. and Mayo, M. (eds) (1995) *Community empowerment*, London: Zed Books.

DWP (Department for Work and Pensions) (2004) *Opportunity for All*, London: The Stationery Office.

Fairbairn-Milson Report (1969) *Youth and community work in the 1970s*, London: HMSO.

FCDL (Federation for Community Development Learning) (2002) *The National Occupational Standards in community development work – Summary*, Sheffield: FCDL.

Francis, D., Henderson, P. and Thomas, D.N. (1984) *A survey of community workers in the United Kingdom*, London: National Institute for Social Work.

Freire, P. (2000) *Pedagogy of the oppressed*, London: Continuum.

Gilchrist, A. (2004) *The well-connected community*, Bristol: The Policy Press.

Gilchrist, A. (2007) *Equalities and communities: Challenge, choice and change*, London: CDF Publications.

Glen, A., Henderson, P., Humm, J., Meszaros with Gaffney, M. (2004) *Survey of community development workers in the UK*, London: CDF Publications.

Henderson, P. and Salmon, H. (1995) *Community organising*, London: CDF.

Henderson, P. and Thomas, D. (2002) *Skills in neighbourhood work*, London: Routledge.

Home Office (2004) *Firm foundations*, London: Home Office.

Ledwith, M. (2005) *Community development: A critical approach*, Bristol: The Policy Press.

Lees, R. and Smith, G. (1975) *Action-research in community development*, London: Routledge and Kegan Paul.

Longstaff, B. (2008a) *Community development challenge: Strategies. Local strategic approaches to community development*, London: CDF.

Longstaff, B. (2008) *Community development challenge: Evaluation. Establishing an outcomes and evidence base*, London: CDF.

Mayo, M. (2005) *Global citizens*, London: Zed Books.

Miliband, D. (2006) NCVO Annual Conference Key Note Speech (www.ncvo-vol.org.uk/events/speeches/?id=2382).

Miller, C. (2008) *Community development challenge: Management towards high standards in community development*, London: CDF.

Paxton, W. and Dixon, M. (2004) *The state of the nation: An audit of injustice in the UK*, London: IPPR.

Popple, K. (1995) *Analysing community work*, Buckingham: Open University Press.

Putnam, R. (2000) *Bowling alone. The collapse and revival of American community*, New York: Simon & Schuster.

Seebohm Report (1968) *Local authority and allied personal social services*, London: HMSO.

Shaw, M. (2004) *Community work: Policy, politics and practice*, Working Paper, University of Hull.

Skeffington Report (1969) *People and planning*, London: HMSO.

Taylor, M. (2003) *Public policy in the community*, Basingstoke: Palgrave Macmillan.

Taylor, M. and West, A. (2001) *Signposts to community development* (3rd edn), London: CDF Publications.

Thomas, D.N. (1983) *The making of community work*, London: George Allen & Unwin.

Younghusband, E. (1959) *Report of the Working Party on social work in local authority health and welfare services*, London: HMSO.

Appendix: The interviewees

Ros Abbott

During the 1970s, Ros was involved in community action in Manchester having trained in youth and community. From 1979, Ros was employed as a community development worker for the Scottish Special Housing Association, based in Glasgow, working on housing and tenant issues. Ros moved to Hull where she was involved in setting up Hull DOC (Developing Our Communities), a community development agency, and worked for many years as a development worker for Hull Federation of Community Organisations; she is currently an outreach worker for Hull Community Network.

Brian Astin

Having worked in Swindon as a community development worker in the early 1970s, Brian left to coordinate the Barton Project in Oxford from the mid-1970s to the mid-1980s, a neighbourhood-based organisation in which he had specific responsibility for overseeing the student unit providing placements for social work students wishing to practise community development. Brian left Oxford to establish and run a social policy unit within the chief executive's department of Oldham Council, focused on anti-poverty work, equalities, voluntary and community sector development. Brian currently oversees corporate strategy and partnerships for Pendle Borough Council.

Alan Barr

Alan started community work in the late 1960s, running Student Community Action and working with the National Union of Students. Alan worked for the Oldham Community Development Project (CDP) for five years during the 1970s before moving to Strathclyde Council to run a fieldwork teaching unit in community work in the Social Work department. He then moved to the University of Glasgow to teach community development before returning to Strathclyde as a principal officer for community development. In the early 1990s he worked with others to establish the Scottish Community Development Centre, where he currently works as a co-director.

Ann Chapman

Ann worked as a generic community worker in the London Borough of Lewisham throughout the 1980s and as the Principal Community Development Officer for Newcastle City Council during the 1990s. With brief spells within the Home Office and also lecturing on community work and women's studies in the academic field, Ann then moved to Kirklees Council in West Yorkshire where she is currently the Principal Community Development Manager. Ann was also vice chair of SCCD (Standing Conference for Community Development), later CDX (Community Development Exchange).

Frances Clarke

Frances Clarke has been involved in Community Links from the late 1970s as a community development worker and manager. Frances began work at Community Links as a community worker and driver of a double-decker community bus. The bus visited a range of high-density estates that led to her work on the Newham Tower Block Tenants Campaign, which later grew into the National Tower Blocks Network. Frances developed Community Links advice and community work programmes over almost 30 years. During that time she introduced a range of innovatory projects including advice work and community development training for local people and advice services in general practitioner (GP) surgeries. She has been responsible for fundraising for this range of activities and for active lobbying for the allocation of resources locally. Frances is now working on the We Are What We Do project, which encourages people to make simple adjustments in their attitudes and behaviour that, if undertaken in sufficient numbers, could make significant changes.

Steve Clarke

Steve began his community development work in South Africa as part of a non-governmental organisation established by students within Witwatersrand University for five years in the mid to late 1960s. Having moved to London and studying community development at the London School of Economics and Political Science (LSE), Steve worked at the Blackfriars Settlement in Southwark before joining the Young Volunteer Force Foundation (YVFF) and working for 12 years in Newport, South Wales. Steve has since taught community development at Swansea University.

Gary Craig

Gary had been involved in Student Community Action at the University of London and later the University of Oxford in the 1960s. He worked in Ghana with Voluntary Services Overseas (VSO) and for the Ghana government, and was then a founder member of the Young Volunteer Force Foundation (YVFF) in 1968 and worked within some of its early projects, including working with Ugandan Asian refugees in a refugee camp during 1971/72. He was employed as part of the Benwell Community Development Project in Newcastle from 1972-78 and then in its successor organisation, a trades union and community resource centre, until 1984. He worked part time for several years to allow him to look after his child, first as a researcher for a radical film company and then as researcher for the Law Centres Federation. In 1988 he went into academic life at the University of Bradford as a research fellow, followed by posts in the Universities of York (research fellow) and Humberside (senior lecturer and then professor). Gary is currently Professor of Social Justice at the University of Hull and Chair of the International Association of Community Development.

Christine Dixon

Christine began work in the early 1970s in a small settlement in the London Borough of Southwark, followed by two years training in community and youth work at Goldsmiths College. From the late 1970s up until 1997, Christine was employed as a community worker for the London Borough of Lambeth, working within a number of different departments over this period and supporting many different communities. Since the late 1990s, Christine has been based within the voluntary sector, for the last year as Temporary Manager for the Waterloo Action Centre.

Charlie Garratt

Having worked with young people in the mid-1970s, Charlie took his first paid community development position, with CDF (Community Development Foundation), as part of the Bedworth Heath Project in 1978, a neighbourhood-based community development project in Warwickshire. Charlie worked at Bedworth Heath for five years before moving on to a CDP in Solihull and later rejoining CDF for 11 years, initially as Head of Consultancies and then as Director of

Community Initiatives. Charlie worked as Chief Executive of People for Action for four years.

Cwti Green

From the late 1970s Cwti worked in a community development role, initially in Aberdeen based in a community centre and working with unemployed young people. From 1980-94, Cwti worked with various church communities and organisations in Aberdeen, Dundee and Glasgow, living and working within the community, and establishing and running a wide variety of community-based projects. Since the mid-1990s, Cwti has been employed as a generic community worker for Community Links in East London, where she has been involved in establishing a breadth of local projects from food co-ops to childcare projects to community singing, and is currently managing a community development training programme.

Tony Herrmann

Tony first became involved with community activities in Scotland and later worked as a community worker in Leeds for over 20 years from the mid-1970s. Initially employed in the voluntary sector, Tony then worked within the social services department for Leeds City Council as a neighbourhood community development worker, and for 13 of these years on the Belle Isle Estate. During this period he was seconded to the University of Leeds for three years to develop and run community-based learning programmes for community groups across Leeds. Tony became the manager of the Community Work Training Company in the late 1990s to further the training and development of community workers and now works as a consultant.

Bob Holman

As Professor of Social Administration at the University of Bath, Bob realised he was too distanced from practice on the ground and left his job to live and work on the Southdown Estate in Bath, setting up the Southdown project, which worked at a neighbourhood level with children and young people. Bob spent the next 10 years living and working on Southdown, followed by a further 10 years living on the Easterhouse Estate in Glasgow, becoming actively involved in the Family Action in Rogerfield & Easterhouse neighbourhood project (FARE).

Dean Huggins

During the early 1980s Dean was involved in work for the Immigration Aid Unit, training and campaigning around immigration and nationality issues. Dean went on to work for the Law Centres Federation in the late 1980s and early 1990s, establishing and supporting law centres around the country. Other work included spells at the National Council for Voluntary Organisations (NCVO), International Voluntary Service and a community resource centre in Coventry. Dean managed the community development team within Newcastle City Council during the 1990s and has since worked in a freelance capacity around equalities, community engagement and community development. Dean is currently chair of Ubuntu, the national network of black and minority ethnic community development workers and activists organised within the Federation for Community Development Learning (FCDL).

Neil Jameson

Neil has three distinct phases to his work, firstly as a worker within a neighbourhood project in Coventry during the 1970s. During the 1980s Neil worked for Save the Children and for the past 15 years has focused on community organising, initiating and now working as Director for the Citizen Organising Foundation and Lead Organiser of London Citizens.

Charlie Jordan

During the mid-1970s Charlie worked as part of the Barton project in Oxford as a community worker before moving to Brighton in 1980 and becoming the only worker for what was then called Brighton and Hove Church & Community Development project (now called People and Churches Together, or PACT), again as a community development practitioner. In his developmental role over 10 years, Charlie established a number of successful organisations including Hangleton and Knoll Community Development Project and what has now become the Brighton Young People's Centre. Today, Charlie divides his time between teaching community development, running action learning programmes and fulfilling his role as chair of the Emmaus community in Brighton.

Barbara Keeley

Barbara has been active in the field of community development and playgroups since 1961, establishing five playgroups between 1962–67 in and around Leighton Buzzard. Barbara was elected to the National Executive of the Preschool Playgroups Association in 1963 and from 1968 was involved in adult education courses for adults running playgroups. Over the years, Barbara has initiated many local community projects including Homestart and a Council of Voluntary Organisations.

John Killion

John began work in 1973 as a detached worker on a council estate in Manchester, employed by Lancashire County Council, followed by many years managing a family centre in Rochdale that brought together children and families work with community development. John later took a role as Team Leader at Rhyl Community Agency before becoming a community development manager for Denbighshire.

Marian McGuiness

Marian began her career in community work in the early 1980s, getting involved as a volunteer for the community where she lived, organising activities and campaigning on issues that affected her family and the community where she lived. She attended Sunderland Polytechnic and gained a youth and community qualification in 1985 and since then she has undertaken a number of different jobs within the statutory and voluntary/community sectors, including: detached youth work with girls and young women, neighbourhood development work, environmental youth development work, community education work and for the past 10 years has had responsibility for developing and managing a project for Barnardo's in the North East, which uses a community development model of practice.

Yousuf Motala

Yousuf had many years of voluntary work experience within Preston before becoming Community Development Officer for Preston & West Lancashire Racial Equality Council, where he worked with excluded groups and communities. Yousuf has worked across Lancashire with ex-offenders and young people at risk and was seconded during this time to the Inner Cities Task Force to develop appropriate strategies to tackle social, education and employment needs within the community. Yousuf has also worked as a tutor on access to primary teaching for minority ethnic communities and is chair of Forward Northwest and a regional black and minority ethnic umbrella network. Yousuf currently works as Principal Community Regeneration Officer with Preston Council with a particular focus on developing partnerships between the voluntary/community sector, statutory sector, faith communities and the private sector.

Paramjit Oberoi

In the late 1970s, Paramjit worked in one of the first community schools, Sidney Stringer, in Coventry, working in particular with Asian, Chinese and Japanese women and children. At the same time, she worked in a hostel established for Asian young women who had run away from home around issues of education, drugs, relationships and family conflict. Paramjit moved to London and worked as a community social worker for Ealing Council in Southall, and was involved on a voluntary basis in the initial establishment of Southall Black Sisters. During the 1980s and 1990s Paramjit worked in roles as a community relations officer for the Council for Racial Equality and then as the principal development officer (ethnic minorities) for Derbyshire Social Services for eight years and as a team manager of a team of community development workers with Nottingham City Council Leisure and Community Services for 10 years. She has also been working as a sessional lecturer and personal tutor for students on the BA (Hons) Applied Community and Youth Studies with the University of Derby for the past 20 years. More recently she has qualified to be a life and business coach and is lecturing on the postgraduate Certificate in Coaching at the University of Derby.

Ashok Ohri

Ashok worked in both Wolverhampton and later Glasgow as a neighbourhood worker during the 1970s for the Young Volunteer Force Foundation (YVFF). In the early 1980s, Ashok was the founder and the first director of the Federation of Community Work Training Groups (now called Federation of Community Development Learning, or FCDL) promoting training and learning opportunities for community workers across the UK. Since the mid-1980s Ashok has worked as a consultant and trainer specialising in the areas of change management, equalities and diversity.

Geeta Patel

Geeta has been active within the sphere of community development for over 20 years. She has particular experience of working with issues relating to domestic violence, anti-racism, housing and health. Through her work with 'Working For Change', a women's training collective, Geeta has both developed and delivered training courses promoting essential skills and knowledge to enable women and black and minority ethnic communities to participate effectively in decision making. In Sheffield, Geeta helped to establish an Asian women's refuge and resource centre. In Wolverhampton she was a founder member of the Asian Women and Diabetes Group. Geeta is currently employed as Senior Health and Social Care Officer for Wolverhampton Voluntary Sector Council, and has co-led work on developing good practice in involving the public in decision making across the city.

David Robinson

While still at school in 1977, together with a friend, David Robinson founded Community Links, a community organisation based in a back room in East Ham, London. In his role as a community worker, David was initially involved in running activities with young people and went on to become Director. Over the years David has been involved in using community experiences as evidence to influence government policy around, for example, benefit payments and volunteering, influencing the design and delivery of government programmes and funding such as New Deal and the Children's Fund and pioneering ground-breaking projects such as Timebank and We Are What We Do.

Greg Smith

Greg began as a trainee community worker with the Renewal Programme in the London Borough of Newham in 1975, an organisation with an evangelical mission and strong commitment to community development. Three years as a lay pastor in nearby Canning Town, which involved informal community work, were followed by a further 20 years living and working within the Green Street area of Newham, initially as a national networker for the Evangelical Coalition for Urban Missions and then work for Aston Charities pursuing his research, community development and inter-faith interests. After a spell of five years doing a series of academic research projects in this field at the University of East London, he has recently returned to community work practice at the Salvation Army's Open Door project in Preston.

Jerry Smith

Jerry became involved in student community action in the late 1960s in Nottingham and then joined the Young Volunteer Force Foundation (YVFF) in 1970 as a community worker on a large council estate in Wolverhampton, followed by three years at the Buttershaw Community Project in Bradford. After stints as a community worker for Nottinghamshire County Council and the Community Projects Foundation (later Community Development Foundation, or CDF), Jerry joined the Nottinghamshire Community Development Project in 1980 until the mid-1980s. Jerry worked for a further 10 years at CDF as a regional manager before joining the Tenant Participation Advisory Service and later working within local government in the North West as a policy and partnerships officer.

Gersh Subhra

Gersh has been involved in youth and community work in Derby and Nottingham, working for various local authorities as well as finding time to qualify as a social worker. Gersh managed community workers in two area teams in Nottingham and was a neighbourhood community worker in Derby. He has been at the University of Derby since 1993 and has taught on the Applied Community and Youth Studies degree as well as helping to develop a Foundation degree in Community Regeneration and Development. Increasingly, Gersh has been involved in external community-based work with a wide variety of agencies and this has included evaluation consultancy, training and project development. He is now the coordinator of a new Centre for Community Regeneration.

Dave Vanderhoven

During the late 1970s and early 1980s, Dave worked with young people in Plaistow in the East End of London, employed by the London Borough of Newham Youth Service. Dave spent much of the 1990s alternating between practising community development within Irish Traveller communities and working extensively with long-term drug users in street-based services and also in rehabilitation, most recently on a freelance basis. Dave is currently studying for a PhD at the University of Sheffield, looking at 'community representation and legitimacy'.

Georgina Webster

For 10 years, from the mid-1970s to mid-1980s, Georgina worked for Lambeth Council in London as a generic community worker responsible for the area of Stockwell. This included one year's leave to study for an MA in Applied Community Studies. Georgina then went to work for Lewisham Council in a policy and training role around community development until the late 1980s. Since then Georgina has worked in a freelance capacity in the field of community development and organisation development as well as acting as chair for SCCD (Standing Conference for Community Development) from 1998-2001. Most recently she works as a neighbourhood renewal adviser for the Neighbourhood Renewal Unit (NRU) with local partnerships. She is a trustee for the Equity Partnership, a Local Government Board (LGB) infrastructure organisation and community centre in Bradford.

Andy Wiggans

Having spent a year in the Inner London Education Authority working with 'school-phobic' children, Andy became a resident community development officer for the social services department in Manchester City Council from 1974-78, which meant him living and working on an estate in the Longsight area of Manchester. He spent the early 1980s running a youth homelessness action research project before joining the Open University for seven years, working on a variety of projects and training initiatives. From the 1990s, Andy worked for Rochdale Council, starting as a principal youth officer and leaving the council in 2005 having spent a number of years as the Director of Recreation and Community Services. Andy currently works freelance, is a trustee for the Wigan Leisure and Culture Trust and is actively involved in thinking and practice around community cohesion and local governance.

Mandy Wilson

In 1982, Mandy joined Community Links as a community worker, initially seconded to work with Newham Tower Blocks Campaign, followed by work on housing, homelessness, women's rights and generic community work. In 1988, Mandy established the Community

Links Training and Development Unit in Sheffield before moving to the Standing Conference for Community Development (SCCD, later the Community Development Exchange, or CDX) in 1992 for a further six years. Since 1998, Mandy has worked as a research and development consultant for Communities & Organisations: Growth & Support (COGS), specialising in community empowerment and regeneration/neighbourhood renewal programmes. Mandy has also been involved in community activity on a voluntary basis throughout this period.

Mel Witherden

From 1974 Mel worked on community enterprise initiatives in Wales, the first 15 years of which were under the auspices of Cwmbran Community Press where he pioneered a community printing and publishing business. Mel spent five years at the Welsh Development Agency in which he set up and ran the Community Enterprise Unit, as well as establishing Community Enterprise Wales. Mel currently works as a consultant and trainer for the charity Community Projects Centre on organisational development and community enterprise projects.

Mark Woodhead

Mark has worked in community development and regeneration, in Yorkshire and elsewhere, since 1982. Over the past 24 years, Mark has practised community development in Leeds, Bradford, Wakefield and Oldham in a range of settings, including a government-funded regeneration programme, a large voluntary organisation and a grant-making trust. He is now employed as Outreach Development Worker for the Active Faith Communities Programme, working in the Wakefield, Kirklees and Calderdale areas. The work involves helping a wide range of faith-based groups to carry out community profiles and to develop projects.

Judy Yacoub

Judy spent many years during the 1980s and 1990s as a campaigner working on transport issues including the M65 and its likely impact on local communities in the North West in terms of housing, the economy and the environment. In the 1990s, Judy worked as a community economic development worker and later as voluntary and community sector coordinator in Pendle. Judy coordinated the development of

Burnley Community Alliance and a £1.5 million capacity building programme, and since 2004 has worked as Chief Executive for the Burnley Community Alliance, involved in developing services and solutions to neighbourhood-based issues.

Index

definitions and use of term 32-3
future predictions 98-101
lessons to guide practice 101-11
see also role of community
development
Community Development Exchange
(CDX) 11, 32, 42, 53
*Strategic framework for community
development* 12-13, 16
Community Development
Foundation (CDF) 11, 12
The community development challenge
13, 16, 32, 34-5, 70, 80, 111
Community Development Journal 9, 16
community development networks
14
Community Development Project
(CDP) 9, 16, 31, 47-9, 93
community development workers
characteristics 91
living in communities 26-8
low numbers historically 19-20, 23
management 24-5
motivation 28-9
national surveys 11, 12, 16, 25, 34-5,
53
professional values 40-3
and state 17-23
community empowerment 13-14, 81,
93, 98-9, 105
empowerment as value 42-3
lacking in target-driven approach
85-6
see also community responsibility
community engagement/involvement
19, 101, 105, 111
and local authorities 70
and policy 13, 17, 35, 49-51, 93-5,
98, 102
and privatisation 99
Community Links project 25-6, 57,
62-3, 63-4, 71, 83-4
community organising movement 14,
16, 46-7, 49, 56-7, 66
and negotiation 70-1, 106
community planning 44, 49, 70-2,
78-9, 103-4
Community Programme 11
Community Projects Foundation 11
community responsibility
self-help and rights 35, 84, 93-4, 105
social pathology model 47, 54, 93

see also community empowerment
community sector 35, 94
community social work 10, 19-20
'community work': use of term 32
Community Work Group 45
competencies *see* skills-based focus
conflict and tension
and Conservative governments 18,
19-20, 76
management of 61
and role of community
development 36-40
conflict of interests 38-40, 40-1
conflict of values 42-3
and local agenda and policy 82-3
supporting community challenges
55-63, 86-7, 90-1, 95-6
Conservative governments 11-12, 18,
19-20, 76
consultation 91
context for community development
17-30
see also policy context
contracts with communities 83, 97
'co-production' 84
Corrigan, Paul 94
councillors' role 68, 100
Craig, Gary 41, 47, 48, 57-8, 61, 109,
110, 119
creating space tactics 62-3
critical thinking and practice 50, 54

D

debate in community development
110-11
democratic participation 93, 94-5,
98-9, 106
Department for Communities and
Local Government (DCLG) 13
see Communities and Local
Government
deprivation *see* poverty and
deprivation
devolution to local level 17, 35, 68,
81, 98
dialogue with authorities 20-1, 63-72,
92
Dixon, Christine 21-2, 24, 77, 87, 119
double devolution 17